Affinity Publisher
for
Fiction Layouts

AFFINITY PUBLISHER FOR
SELF-PUBLISHING - BOOK 1

M.L. HUMPHREY

SELECT TITLES BY M.L. HUMPHREY

CONTENTS

CONTENTS (CONT.)

CONTENTS (CONT.)

INTRODUCTION

This book is a guide to walk users through how to create a print layout for a fiction title in Affinity Publisher.

When I first started self-publishing I just used Microsoft Word to format both my ebooks and paperbacks. And there's a certain advantage to using Word that I still think makes it a valid choice for new self-publishers. Most people are already comfortable with it, and as long as you know how to use Styles and Breaks you can put together an acceptable book.

There are obviously a few tricks involved when it comes to using Word for print, and I definitely had a few moments of struggling with page numbering and tables of contents over the years.

For example, if you are doing non-fiction and want a blank even-numbered page before your next chapter start that requires using a section break and then removing the page number in that section only and making sure the page number didn't get edited on any other pages. Annoying, but doable.

So if you're brand new to self-publishing and drowning in everything you need to learn to publish your books, then maybe stick with Word. Or, get Vellum. That's where I went next in my quest to create pretty ebooks and paperbacks. I'm not even a Mac user, but it was worth it to me to spend $250 to get a used Mac to use Vellum on my books and I still use it for my ebooks.

Vellum is a nice, easy-to-use formatting option for both ebook and print. And, trust me, I looked into all those other options that people suggested at the time for ebooks, but Vellum won hands down because it didn't require a ton of expertise to use.

When they came out with their print option I was happy to use that for my novels.

(I never used it for most of my non-fiction because they just didn't have the level of control I want for complex non-fiction that includes sub-sections and images and indexes, etc.)

So, again, if you're new to self-publishing and want to invest in one single software to get started, I'd actually recommend Vellum. It's great for ebook formatting and it'll do the basics for print formatting which is what most self-published authors need when they're getting started.

But if you're like me, you're ultimately going to want more control. I already mentioned my issues with respect to non-fiction and even on the fiction side I personally have an issue with how they handle widows and orphans.

Now, the old-school recommendation is to move to Adobe InDesign at that point. But I did a trial and I didn't like it. I also hate subscription-based software with a passion. Which ultimately led me to Affinity, and Affinity Publisher in particular. One flat fee and a great product.

I've now used it to format probably a hundred or more titles and am still very pleased with it. But there is a learning curve involved.

You can do what I did to learn Affinity Publisher, which is watch the videos they have for free on their website (https://affinity.serif.com/en-us/tutorials/publisher/desktop/), search for help on the internet, and use good old-fashioned trial and error.

That works if you're the type of personality I am who likes to learn that way. I think their videos are excellent. My problem with that approach was that the videos weren't in the order I needed them to be. I didn't have the background to put them into context and some of the videos I most needed to start with—like Master Pages—were much further down on the page so I thought I wasn't going to be able to learn from them.

Another learning option, of course, is this book or the videos I put together on the same topic. The advantage to having this book is that I will walk through from start to finish how I put together a fiction book so everything is in the order (for the most part) that works best for fiction layouts.

I say for the most part because ideally you have all of your Master Pages and Text Styles set up before you begin (and you will after we create your first book), but for me the most intuitive way to build that first book involves a little bit of back and forth setting all of that up. So if that occasional "let's go back and add this bit" moment will throw you then I still may not be the best choice for you.

But if you stick with me, then by the time you finish this book and/or watch the videos, you should have your first fiction book ready to go and have a firm grasp of all of the steps and skills that are needed to create a basic fiction book that includes an accent font, a main body font, and an image that is used in the front matter and chapter headings.

(By the way, a video course that covers the same material as this book is available at ml-humphrey.teachable.com. There's a discount code available at the back of the book for half off the course price. You can also buy a template similar to what we're going to create here through my Payhip store at payhip.com/mlhumphrey, but I do think going through the book and building your first book from scratch is the best way to learn these skills.)

So it's your choice how to learn Affinity Publisher. However you do it, I think it's well worth learning.

Also, if you're new to my books, be advised up front that I am focused in on what you need to know to get this particular job done, so don't expect 100% mastery of every little bell and whistle the program offers. I personally find books like that overwhelming and like to just get right to the meat of what I need to know, but that may not work for all personalities.

Also, the folks at Affinity are continually improving their programs, so what I say now could change. For example, there have been times when I went looking for a functionality in the Affinity suite and it didn't exist but then it was there in the next release. So this is written as of this moment in time (September 2021).

Another note. I am working on a PC so the screenshots you'll see are based on that version of Affinity. Where I use Ctrl shortcuts on an Apple you'd use Command instead.

Finally, I'm going to assume in this book that you can handle the basics of working in a Microsoft Office-style program that has dropdowns and dialogue boxes, etc. (If you don't know what Control shortcuts (like Ctrl + C to copy), dialogue boxes, dropdowns, etc. are then maybe start with my book *Word for Beginners* which defines all of those things. It's obviously for a different software, but that basic functionality and terminology holds across programs and having at least that level of understanding is kind of essential for what we're going to do here.)

I'm also going to assume that you know the basics of formatting for print. If you are brand new to print and don't know anything about anything then maybe check out *Print Books for Beginners* which is available for purchase on my Payhip store in ebook format. (I unpublished it on the wide platforms because the platform information was changing too fast, but the discussion in there about formatting a print book remains unchanged. I'll probably also put up a short video course on that at some point so keep an eye out for that in the Teachable store as well. Check my website mlhumphrey.com for the latest information.)

Alright then. Let's dive in and create a fiction layout for print using Affinity Publisher.

A BRIEF INTRODUCTION TO AFFINITY

The Affinity suite of products can be located at affinity.serif.com. They offer three products, Affinity Photo, Affinity Designer, and Affinity Publisher. Each one has a free trial option so you can see what they're like to work with before you spend your money.

As of the date I'm writing this, each of the three products costs $54.99 in the United States. If you want to wait around they do seem to put them on sale at various points in time throughout the year, but I think that's a very reasonable price for what they offer since it's a one-time payment and you get full updates for that cost.

Again, keeping in mind that I am a self-published author and not a design guru, this is my personal rundown of the three products.

Publisher, which is what we're going to cover in this book, allows you to do multiple-page layouts where text flows across pages. It's also what allows you to insert a table of contents or an index. There are basic design options as well. You can insert images onto pages very easily, for example.

According to their website, Publisher allows you to "combine your images, graphics and text to make beautiful layouts ready for publication."

I also create my covers and advertising images using Publisher. But I will put a little asterisk here because the type of covers I create are basic text and image placement. If you need to do photo manipulation, then you need one of the other Affinity products. Publisher is for putting components into a final layout, not for creating those components.

Designer is the one I use the least and may not even need although I do have it. According to their website it's for creating concept art, print projects, logos, icons, UI designs, mock-ups and more. I can't remember the last time I actually dipped into Designer, but I'd say this is where you combine multiple layers to create really complex images.

Photo is the other Affinity product I do use on occasion. This is the product you need, if, for example, you're going to use layer masks to make your title text on a cover more visible against a background that has a lot of detail. (If you want to learn how to do that and all sorts of other cool things, check out the NeoStock cover design course at https://www.neo-stock.com/core-skills-photoshop-video-training. The course is done in Photoshop but I was able to translate what he discusses there to Affinity.)

You will also use Photo if you ever want to use a mockup file like the ones available for free from CoverVault (https://covervault.com/) that let you create a 3D image of your cover. Even though they're built for Photoshop, Affinity can work with them. Just be sure to change your General Preferences so that "Import PSD smart objects where possible" is checked.

* * *

One of the nice things about Affinity is that if you have all three you can move between Publisher, Designer, and Photo within the same file. They call them personas and they are available in the top left corner of the workspace. So any time you're in Publisher, for example, and you need to do something that's only possible in Designer or Photo, you can just click on the "persona" for the other program and the workspace will change and give you the options for that program without you having to close the file or import or export.

Now that you have that background, we're going to focus in on Publisher, because that's all you should need for putting together a beautiful fiction layout for print.

GETTING STARTED WITH PUBLISHER

Okay then. I'm going to assume here that you've gone to the Affinity website and downloaded Affinity Publisher and have opened it.

If you have a lot of fonts, like I do thanks to my font addiction which has been fed by cheaply-priced Design Cuts bundles (https://www.designcuts.com/), then Affinity may be slow to load.

My computer is pretty fast, but on the one where I have all of my fonts accessible, it takes about ten times longer to load Affinity as it does on my computer where I moved the fonts I really don't use into a different folder.

So if Affinity is slow to start and you have lots of fonts and that bugs you, move the fonts you don't use to a different folder.

Once Affinity loads, you should see something similar to this:

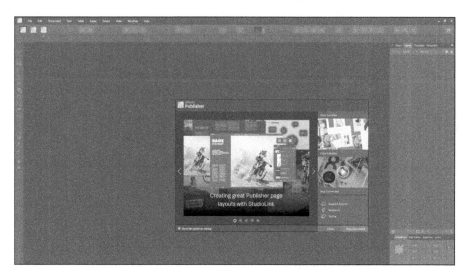

Personally I like to set my workspace up a little differently, so let's cover that next. Click on Close to get rid of that Affinity Publisher welcome screen and then let's go set up your studio presets.

SET UP YOUR WORKSPACE

I prefer to arrange my workspace differently depending on whether I'm doing a cover design or working on the interior of a book. Especially since I do a lot of non-fiction interiors that involve images and indexes, etc. So before we begin I want to walk you through how to make your workspace look like the one I'm going to be using from here on out.

To do that, you have to understand that Affinity works with what they call studios. The full range of studios can be found by going to View at the top of the screen, clicking on that, and then taking your mouse down to Studio. This brings up a secondary dropdown menu with a number of listed options.

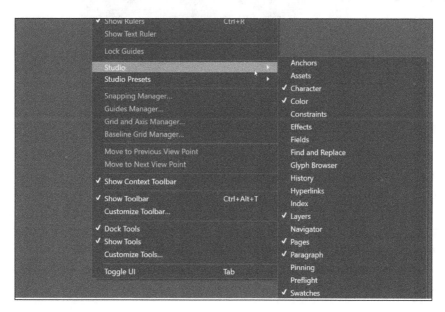

You can see that some, like Character and Color, are checked. And some, like Preflight, are not. The ones that are checked are already visible in your workspace. The ones that are not checked are not visible by default. Character is on the top right in the default view and Color is on the bottom right in the default view, for example, but to use Preflight you'd have to specifically open it.

A studio is basically a task pane that you can click on to see various options related to that topic. We're not going to dig too deep into that right this second, because you're going to learn all about those options later by seeing and doing. For now, just accept that each studio gives you different options and that for creating a print interior I want you to have certain studios available in your workspace.

Now it's time to arrange our workspace with the studios we're going to use and to put them where I find they work the best for me.

The first thing I want you to do is go to your main workspace and on the top right-hand side find the tab for Pages. Left-click on it and drag it over to the left-hand side of your workspace. If you drag it to a point where it overlaps with the left-hand set of menu choices it should flash blue and have an outline.

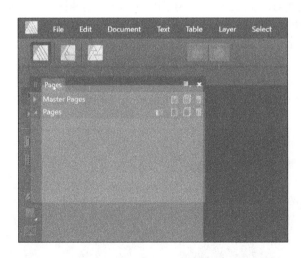

Let go at that point and the studio should move to that side of your workspace and "dock" so that it's fixed to that point now.

Next I want you to add the Find and Replace, Table of Contents, Index, Preflight, Fields, and Text Styles studios. For each one, go to View, go down to Studio, and then select it. This will either add that studio as a tab next to your existing studios or it will open as a standalone dialogue box on top of the workspace.

If they open as standalone dialogue boxes, you'll end up with something that looks like this with all of the studios open on top of your workspace:

We need to place those studios somewhere we can access them easily but where they aren't in the way.

Left-click on Text Styles and drag it over to where the Layers, Character, and Paragraph studios are on the top right-hand side of your screen. When you do so it should get added to that set of tabs. Drag it to the end and let go. It should now look like this:

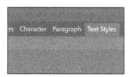

See how Text Styles is listed at the end of that row of options? Now add Fields to the same section.

Next, click and drag Find and Replace next to Pages so that you have two tabs in that section. Then do the same for Table of Contents, Index, and Preflight.

When you're done, you'll have a workspace that looks like this where I currently have the Pages studio selected on the left-hand side and the Layers studio selected on the right-hand side.

You can click on each tab to see the options available for that particular studio, but can only see the options for one studio in each section at a time. That's why I like to have my Pages studio on the left-hand side so that it's almost always visible while I'm working in my text studios on the right-hand side.

This is how I personally like to have my workspace set up when working with print layouts, but you can set it up any way you want. If you're doing only fiction, for example, you may not need to have an index so you may want to close that out.

Or if you don't plan to have a table of contents (which our example isn't going to have) you may want to close that. But these are the studios I find myself using the most when doing print layouts and they're the ones you'll see in the screenshots in the rest of this book.

When you exit Affinity and come back in, it will give you the last workspace layout you were using. So if you only have one way in which you want to use Affinity, you can simply set it up and exit and Affinity will retain that layout.

For cover design, however, I use a very different layout from my print design layout. Rather than recreate this layout each and every time, I use studio presets that let me move back and forth between my two workspaces.

To save a layout as a studio preset, click on the View option in the top menu, go to Studio Presets, and choose Add Preset.

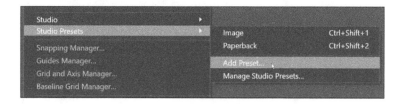

This will bring up a dialogue box which asks you to provide a name for your preset studio layout. I call mine Paperback. So type that into the box and then choose OK.

If you then go back to the View, Studio Presets option, you can see all of your available presets. So in the image above you can see that I have Paperback and Image to choose from.

To change over to your preferred preset, simply click on the one you want. Or you can see in the image above that Affinity automatically assigns each preset a Control shortcut of Ctrl + Shift + [a number].

For the curious, this is how I have the top right corner for my Image workspace arranged:

I've moved the Color, Swatches, and Text Frame studios up and also added the Glyph Browser. I have Transform by itself down below and have nothing on the left-hand side.

The main focus for me when working on images is the Layers studio. For book formatting it's the Pages studio.

One more thing before we move on from studio presets and that's how to change one. As far as I can tell there is not a save feature for when you update existing presets, but what does work is to save a new preset using the old name.

When you do that and click OK it then asks if you want to replace the existing studio preset that has that name and you can say Yes. Done.

Alright. Now that we've set up our workspace, it's time to move on to setting up our file.

SET UP A NEW FILE TEMPLATE

The next step is to set up your new file for a print paperback. Depending on the type of book you're writing this will vary. So, for example, when I publish a novel I use a 5.25 by 8 inch size with certain margin settings. But when I publish that same novel in large print I use a 6 by 9 inch size with different margins. And when I publish non-fiction computer books I use 7.5 by 9.25 inch.

When in doubt about your settings, I always recommend starting with the print book templates provided by Amazon. They download as a Word file, but then you can open that file and go to Page Layout-> Margins-> Custom Margins to see how they've set up their margins for that specific size.

Keep in mind that print books use something called mirrored margins, meaning that the outer left and outer right margins are the same and the inner left and inner right margins are the same. The inner margin tends to be larger and to also include what's called a gutter which allows room for binding the pages together without cutting off the text.

If you're going to do this more than once you can create a preset for each size. (Although what I tend to do is open the last book of that size that I did and just delete out the text from the last book and replace it with my new text. I do this because then the master pages, etc. are all the way I want them already. But for ad templates I do have presets, simply because I'm too lazy to remember all the various sizes that are required for all the different ad types.)

Anyway. Go to File-> New or if you just opened Affinity click on New Document from the welcome screen. This will bring up the New Document dialogue box. There are default print sizes listed, but I don't use them because they're not what I need.

For example, here I've clicked on Print and then Letter and you can see on the right-hand side that this is for an 8.5 x 11 inch document with a DPI of 300, that the unit size is in inches, that it is a portrait orientation and images are going to be embedded and it's also one page. The color format is also RGB/8. Scroll down more and you'll see information about the margins and any bleed.

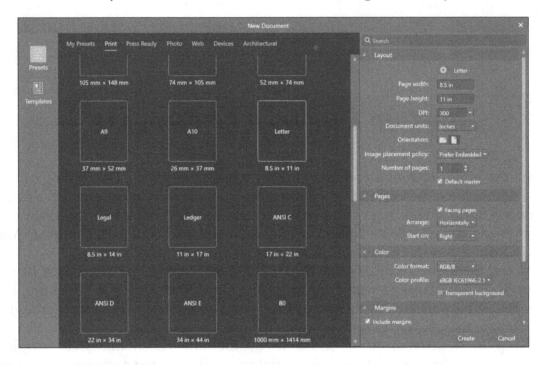

What I recommend is finding this existing template or another that's in inches and then editing it. We're going to do that to create something that will work for a 5.25 x 8 inch book.

First, click onto the 8.5 x 11 inch template. Next, click into page width and change that to 5.25 and then tab to the next field. (As soon as you do that the Layout name just above that field will change to Custom, because it's no longer that existing template.)

Next, change the page height to 8 and make sure the DPI is 300 or more. For fiction this isn't as important, but if you want to put your cover image at the front of the book or if you want an image for each chapter start or for your section dividers then you ideally want this set to 300 DPI or more. If it isn't the image may be blurry. (Not horribly so, but it's easy enough to address here so why not do it?)

Plus it saves you getting an alert from IngramSpark when you upload your file. (Assuming that the images you place remain 300 DPI after you've placed them. Affinity can't fix the nature of a small image.)

OK. 5.25, 8, 300 (or a little more if you want), inches, portrait. (If you ever do a picture book or something like that you may need to change this to landscape, but even then it may be fine.)

Image placement can go either way. For fiction it only matters if you plan to include an image, which our template does, so this setting does matter to us. I'm going to use Linked.

Linking the image saves file size and if you use a handful of different images in a file Affinity is going to ask if you'd rather link than embed anyway. Also, if you're linked instead of embedded, Affinity will warn you when you update the image outside of the program and ask if you want to update the image within your file which can be a useful reminder that you need to do so. And it makes it easier to swap out an image if you use it multiple times in your document and choose to use a different one later.

One drawback to linked is that if you move the image from where it's saved and don't update you'll have a blurred space where that image should be instead of the image itself in your document.

Next, I always set it to have a number of pages of 1. I then add more pages using Master Pages, which we'll discuss soon.

And you want facing pages, arranged horizontally, that start on the right.

I recommend using Gray/8 as your color. This will transform any color image you put into the document into a grayscale image which is what you're going to want for most titles. (As a print-on-demand self-publisher the cost of a color book is generally too high to bother with.) Gray/16 can work as well, but interestingly enough last time I checked Ingram wanted 8 not 16. This is another one that's really only relevant if you use images.

Margins. For a 5.25 by 8 book I have mine set to .9 inch for the inner margin, .6 inch for the outer margin, and .76 inches for the top and bottom margins.

I also have bleed set on my books of .125 inches for each side. To be honest, I'm not sure I need it and I'm pretty sure the export option I choose drops it out. But I just keep it there in case.

(The only time bleed really comes up is if you're using Affinity Publisher with one of the KDP cover templates, because they do have bleed and you do need to remember to export your file with bleed included or else Amazon will tell you that the cover isn't the right size.)

Back to this new document. If you're not going to use it again, click Create and it will create a new document for you using those parameters.

If you do want to use it again, then you need to create a preset template. To do that, go back to the top of your options and click on the + sign next to Custom. This will add the preset you just created to the My Presets section with a name of Unnamed 1 (or whatever number you're up to if you haven't named your presets).

Right-click on that thumbnail and choose Rename Preset and type in the name you want. Be sure to choose a name that is descriptive enough that you'll know what the file is. I prefer to include size information and purpose.

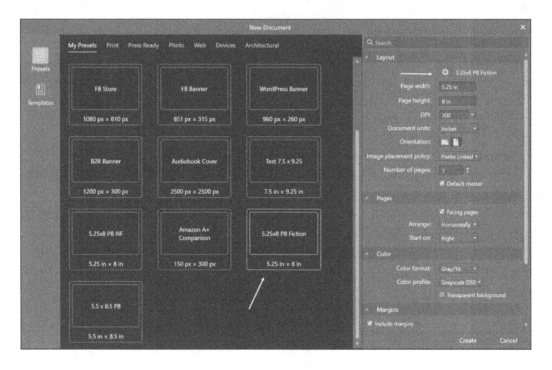

In the image above you can see my new 5.25x8 PB Fiction preset in the bottom right corner and that that name is also showing on the top right-hand side above all of my parameters.

As a side note, you can see the other templates I have in there. I have presets for Facebook ads, ebook covers, BookBub ads, Facebook banners, etc. Creating these in advance makes it much easier to just open Affinity and create a new ad without having to go dig for the required dimensions.

Before we move on from here, let me just touch on large print for a minute.

For my large print books I use a 6 by 9 size. So inches are 6 and 9. And I increase the size of my margins to a 1 inch inner margin, a .75 inch outer margin, and a .9 inch top and bottom margin. Otherwise, the settings remain unchanged.

Okay.

Once you're done with your settings, click on Create. You will get something that looks like this.

It should look like a page of the book you want to create. That blue border in the center is the area where we've told Affinity text will go. The white space around it is the space for your margins. That blue border in the black space around the perimeter is the area for the bleed which, as I mentioned before, I'm not sure you actually need but it doesn't hurt to include.

It can be tempting at this point to try to type into that space. The next step is to add text, right? But no. We still need to lay groundwork with our Master Pages and Text Styles.

MASTER PAGES

For me, master pages are the core of what makes using Affinity Publisher so much better than using Word for print formatting.

Master pages are basically templates that you create that include your page numbering, your headers, your footers, any images you want on the page, and your text placement.

I create a master page for every type of two-page spread I need in a book.

Applying master pages is probably 75% of the formatting work of creating a book. Combine that with text styles, which we'll talk about shortly, and you're probably 90% of the way there.

Ideally.

For the fiction book we're going to create here, I have nine master pages. There's the title page, the also by page, the copyright and chapter start page, and the about the author page. And then there are the master pages for the main body text which include all of the combinations of chapter start and text (text and chapter start, chapter start and text, no text and chapter start, text and text, and text and no text).

For any given book you may not use all of those, but it's nice to have them if you need them and they're pretty easy to put together. (I think you can actually do your master pages in one-page spreads instead which would mean having a text, a chapter start, and a no text master page, but then you'd also have to apply them one at a time and I don't think it saves all that much effort so we're going to be building two-page master pages here.)

It probably sounds a little complicated right now, so let's just dive in and start building. I'm going to assume from here on out that you built your workspace to look like mine and I'll give directions based on that fact. If you didn't, then you'll need to adjust accordingly.

So.

Go to the top left corner of your workspace where we pinned the Pages studio and click on it. You should see two sections, one for Master Pages and one for Pages. Click on Master Pages to expand that section. It should look like this once you do:

Double-click on that Master A thumbnail in the Master Pages section and you will see that master in the main workspace where you can now edit it.

But first, go back to the Master A thumbnail and click on its name. This should highlight the name in blue. Type in the name you want for this master page and click enter. I'm going to name this first master page "Simple Title Page."

If your view has small thumbnails in it where the name is off to the side instead of below the thumbnail, I'd recommend you change that. To do so, be sure that you have the Pages studio selected and then go to the top right corner of that section (right above the trash can) and click on the image with four lines and a little dropdown arrow on the right-hand side.

This will bring up a dropdown menu where you can change the option from Small to Large.

Much better. Much easier to see the difference between your master pages with just a glance.

Of course, right now, there's only one master page and it's blank so there's not much to see. Let's change that.

SIMPLE TITLE PAGE

Go to the main workspace where you should see a larger version of your master page. (If not, double-click on the thumbnail to bring it up.)

Right now, this page has no elements on it. You can see two blue borders that designate our "text area", but the page itself is not yet set up with text frames to hold text. It's more like a sketch of our basic format so we know where to place our elements, but none of what you see right now will appear on your final document. And if we added text directly onto this page right now it would not in any way be constrained to those text areas.

That's what we're doing when we build master pages. We're adding the elements that we want to use on each page. For this simple title page, that's going to be a text frame and an image. What we ultimately want on this page should look like this:

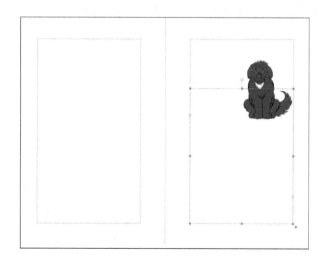

Obviously you can add whatever design elements you want. For this guide, I'm going to walk you through a fairly simple layout that I've used in the past for my cozy mystery series that includes a few little embellishments that highlight what you can do with Affinity but that also doesn't take much effort.

So from here on out I'll be recreating the layout for *A Dead Man and Doggie Delights*, the first book in that series, so you can see what we're doing applied to real content. The image I use in those books is that Newfoundland dog that you see in the screenshot above.

To create the title page, the first thing we want to do is add the text frame. To do this, click on the capital T on the left-hand-side panel of options to select the Frame Text Tool. This will let you create a box on the page where you can then place text.

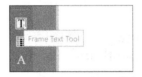

After you select the tool, when you hold your cursor over the workspace you'll see that you now have a little T in a box hanging out next to your cursor. Go to the right-hand page of your workspace and left-click and drag to form a text frame that aligns with the blue outline on the right, left, and bottom edges.

I click on the left-hand edge of the frame and then drag down and over.

As you drag the text frame into place, you will see green or red lines when the frame aligns with your existing boundaries. So in the picture below you can see that there is a red line where I've dragged the frame down to the bottom boundary and a green one along the right side. This means I've created a text frame that fills the space I wanted to use for placing text in my document.

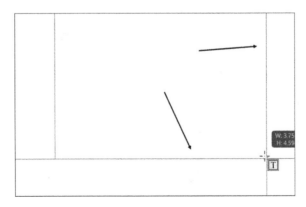

If you don't see any red or green lines as you drag your text frame into alignment, then you need to turn on Snapping. This can be done by going to the top menu and clicking on the dropdown arrow next to the image that looks like a red horseshoe magnet. In the menu that appears when you do that make sure that the Enable Snapping box at the top is checked.

For the main text on a page, you want any text frames that you place in your master pages to line up with the template boundaries we established for our text. (Remember, this is for creating a basic fiction book layout. If this were a magazine spread, that might not be the case.)

If you don't get it right immediately, that's okay. You can always click on the text frame again to select it, and then click and drag from the blue circles along the perimeter to resize the frame.

Below I've created a text frame that goes too far to the right and the bottom to show how this works.

I clicked on the frame, and you can see its outline using the blue circles in the corners and along each edge. It's a little confusing because the line for the text area in the template is also blue, but those circles along the edge and at the corners are the best indicators of which lines belong to the text frame.

The text frame I inserted is aligned with the text area on the left-hand side, but not on the other three sides.

To align the text frame with the bottom and right-hand edges, I can left-click on the circle in the bottom right corner and drag left and up until I see the red and green lines that tell me I'm aligned with the template frame like in the screenshot I initially showed you above.

When you get the text frame aligned with the text area in the template, the blue circles will also turn red or green.

Once you do this, let up on the left-click, and your text frame will be aligned with the underlying template frame.

Now we have something else to fix.

The text frame I just drew isn't the height I want for this page. I don't want it all the way to the top, but I do want it to be taller than this. And because I want to make sure that I use the same height across my master pages for visual continuity, I'm going to adjust this via the Transform studio.

The Transform studio is in the bottom right corner. Click on that tab. The current width of my text frame (W) is 3.75 and the current height (H) is 4.594.

What we want to fix is the H value.

I want a height of 4.75, so I click into the H box and I change the value to what I want and then hit enter.

The increase in height was added to the bottom of the frame, which means it's no longer aligned with my template. I can easily fix this by clicking and dragging the text frame up so that it's within the boundaries of the template once more.

How to do this will depend on whether you have the Move Tool selected or a different tool selected.

You likely have the Text Frame Tool still selected, which means you can hold your mouse over the top edge of the text box until it turns into a four-sided arrow and then click and drag the text frame into alignment.

If you instead had the Move Tool selected then the four-sided arrow won't appear, but you can left-click anywhere on the text frame and drag into place.

(Reminder: click and drag means you left-click and hold that left-click as you move your cursor which should also move the selected object. Also, from here on out, if I just say to click, assume that means left-click.)

If you don't want to also include an image on your title page, that would be it. You now have a master page where you can type in your title on the right-hand page and there will be no headers, footers, page numbers, etc. that appear on that page or the opposite page.

But let's go ahead now and add an image. As I showed you above, I have a simple black and white image of the Newfoundland dog I use on my covers that I want to add to the right-hand corner of that text frame.

To add your image, click on the icon with a picture of mountains on it from the left-hand set of options. (It will show as the Place Image Tool if you hover your mouse over it.)

This will bring up an Open dialogue box where you can then navigate to and select the image you want to use. Once you've done so, click Open.

For me when I did that it automatically put the image in the text frame because I hadn't clicked away from it.

But I don't actually want that. I want my image to be separate from my text frame.

If this happens to you, go to the Layers studio on the top right-hand side of the screen and click on the arrow on the left-hand side for that text frame layer to expand it.

When you expand the text frame layer, you'll see a separate layer for the image that's shown as a subset of the text frame layer.

(I've made the thumbnails here large so they're easier to see. It's the same method as we used for the Pages studio thumbnails.)

Because I don't want that image as a sub item in the text layer, I need to unpin the image.

If you look very closely at the image layer, you'll see that on the right-hand side there is a checkbox. And to the left of that is a white box with lines around it. (It's kind of hard to see, but it's there. I have an arrow pointing to it in the screenshot above.) Click on that white box with lines.

This will open the Pinning studio. From there click on Unpin.

When you unpin the image, this will separate the image layer from the text frame layer. They will both still show in the Layers studio, but will now show as independent of one another.

(You could have also just clicked on the image layer, opened the Pinning studio using the View-> Studio option in the top menu and unpinned that way as well.)

* * *

Of course, it is possible to not have to go through that whole unpinning mess. That happened to me because I was still clicked onto that text frame layer when I tried to insert the image. But I wanted to walk through how to fix it in case it happened to you, too, since it was the default outcome based on the steps we'd already followed.

(I can't tell what will go wrong for you in your book creation process, but I can pretty much guarantee that something will go wrong. Don't panic when that happens. Affinity has good help and internet searches for Affinity instructions also work well. And you can always reach out to me if you get stuck, too.)

* * *

Okay. To avoid that process of having to unpin your image from the Text Frame, before you insert the image click on the Move Tool black arrow at the top of the left-hand set of icons. Then click on the image tool. That will ensure that you're not still in the text frame tool when you insert the image.

If you then click on the Place Image Tool, rather than Affinity inserting the image for you, you'll see a weird little shape next to your cursor that looks like an arrow pointing down at a blue and white circle.

Left-click and drag on the right-hand side of your workspace where you want to place the image. As you click and drag, you should see your image appear on the page. Drag until it's approximately the size you want.

The screenshot above shows the image as well as the cursor in the bottom-right corner.

The image should insert proportionately, meaning it won't stretch or skew as you put the image into your document, and it should appear as its own standalone layer in the Layers studio.

Once the image is inserted into the document you can move it around by left-clicking on it and dragging or left-clicking on the layer in the Layers studio and then left-clicking and dragging.

Once the image has been clicked on you can also use the arrow keys to move it around rather than dragging with the mouse.

To change the dimensions you can drag from the corner or use the Transform section.

If you want to keep the height and width proportionate, the best bet is to use the Transform section and click on the Lock Aspect Ratio option to the right side of the W and H boxes. It looks like two little links connected by a center bar. When it's locked it will have lines going between the W and H boxes and any change to W will also change H or vice versa.

You can use the blue circles around the perimeter of the image to change the size, however doing so will stretch the image out of shape. (Remember, just like in Microsoft Office, Ctrl + Z, Undo, is your friend.)

If you think you accidentally stretched an image, but it's not blatantly obvious you can check that in the Preflight studio that we placed on the top left-hand side. According to Affinity you can use Shift and double-click one of the side handles to return the image to a proportionate size, but I just adjust the image until that warning in the Preflight studio goes away.

I want to position this image so that it is aligned on the right-hand side of the text area and centered along the top edge of my text frame. Like so:

See the red line through the center and the green line along the right-hand edge? That's what I want.

Okay. So that's it. That's the first master page. We have our text frame and our image. But no actual text. And here's why:

In any master page, you don't want to include text or images on that master page that you wouldn't want to see on every single page in your document that uses that master page.

So since the only text I want on this page is the book title and that will vary each time I create a book for this series, I don't want to put the book title on my master page. On the next master page we create, the Also By page, I am going to have the text because it's the same across all of the books. But for this page, no.

(It's not the end of the world if you do put the title on the page now, you'll just have to replace it in the Pages section each time, which could impact carrythrough of any updates you make to that master page.)

ADD TITLE PAGE TO THE DOCUMENT

Once you have your title page ready, it's time to add it to your actual document. You do this in the Pages section of the Pages studio.

Let's look at that now. This is the Pages studio with both our Master Pages and Pages versions of this first page.

Right now, they look the same.

In the Master Pages section we have the Simple Title Page we just created. You can't see the text box, but it's there. You can see the image we inserted. Same for the first page in the Pages section which by default uses this master page because it's the only one

In the Pages section you only see the right-hand side, because when we set up our document we told Affinity to start the document on the right-hand side.

Now it's time to add our book title which we want to do in the document we're creating, so in the Pages section. Double-click on that single-page thumbnail.

The page that you now see in the workspace should be that first single page from the Pages section.

We want to add text to it. To do so, click on the A from the left-hand menu which is the Artistic Text Tool. Next, click into the text frame on the page and type in your title. Like so:

But that doesn't work at all, does it? The text is way too small for the space. Plus I want to use a different font.

Use Ctrl + A to select all of the text you just typed. Now go to the top left menu and you'll see dropdowns where you can change the font, font weight, and font size.

(If you don't see the font dropdown options make sure you have the text layer selected as well as the text tool selected.)

Okay. For this series I use a font called Brushability Sans and on this page I like to use the Light weight in a 30 point size. Font selection works just like it would in Word. You can start typing the font name into the dropdown menu field or scroll down to the one you want.

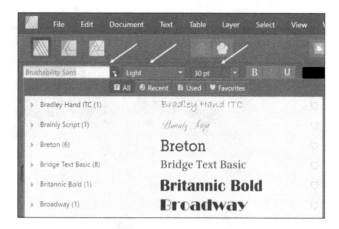

(You probably won't have Brushability Sans as a font choice but if you want practice changing out your fonts, you can use Calibri instead.)

After I make that change, I now have this:

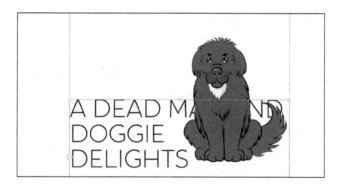

It still has an issue though, right? Because the text is still going across the image and you can't read it.

At this point it might be tempting to just use Enter to create line breaks to get that text to no longer touch the image we inserted. But you don't have to do that.

And you don't *want* to either, because if you do that you're fixing the problem once with a manual solution. Better to fix it forever with an automated solution.

So to fix this, go back to the Master Page section. Double-click on the thumbnail for the title page, click on the Move Tool, and then click on the image or just click on the layer for the image in the Layers studio.

Now go to the top set of menu options and click on the Show Text Wrap Settings icon (indicated by the arrow at the top of the screenshot below). This will bring up the Text Wrap dialogue box.

In this particular case, the options we want to click on are a Wrap Style of Tight and then Wrap To Largest Side. (See arrows above.)

What that's going to do is wrap the text around the image on the left-hand side because that's the side that has the most space, and it's going to keep the text close to the image and still on the same line but without overlapping it.

As you can see in that dialogue box, there are other options available. We'll use one of them on the next master page.

And here's what we get automatically in our document as a result of that change:

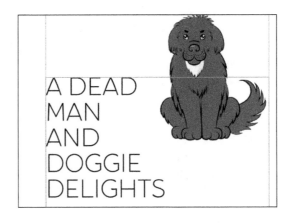

Now, why did we do this in the master? One, because Affinity won't let us do it on an actual page since the image was originally placed onto the master, so we had no real choice. But, two, because that means this formatting we just applied will always apply to the use of this master page. You won't have to think about it again. Every title you type into that title page in the Pages section, the text will automatically flow around the image.

(You may need to think about the optics of how it flows. With my cozy mystery series I found that a title later in the series that had longer words in it flowed differently and I had to adjust my font size to make it look good, but the actual flowing of the text around the image will not be an issue again.)

So that was our first master page completed.

A quick note before we move on.

While you're working on your document, if you ever want to see what a page is going to look like when it's printed without having to generate a PDF, look at that page in the Pages section. The workspace will show lines that aren't going to appear in the final, but the thumbnails should always look like your final product.

Okay. That probably seemed like a lot, but the good news is you only have to create this once for each series and if you stick to a similar layout for your other series it's not a lot of work to update. Let me show you just how easy it can be.

CHANGE IMAGE

Let's say that for another series I don't want a Newfoundland dog on the title page, but instead I want a bulldog in a top hat. By the time we're done here we'll have seven different master pages that use that image. But the nice thing is you don't have to change each of those seven pages individually. You can use the resource manager and change them all at once.

To do that, go to Document at the top of the screen and choose Resource Manager from the dropdown menu. This will bring up the Resource Manager dialogue box.

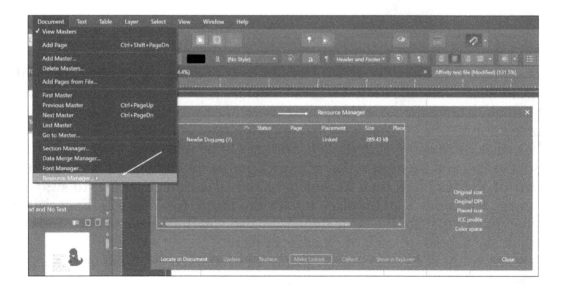

If your images are linked and you've used multiple versions of an image, you will see the image listed with an arrow next to it. You can click on that arrow to see each usage of the image. But you can also, for our purposes, just click on that row for the image you want to replace and then click on the Replace option down below.

Navigate to where the new image you want to use is located, click on it, and click on Open.

Your document should now have the new image in place of the old one in each location it was used as you can see here:

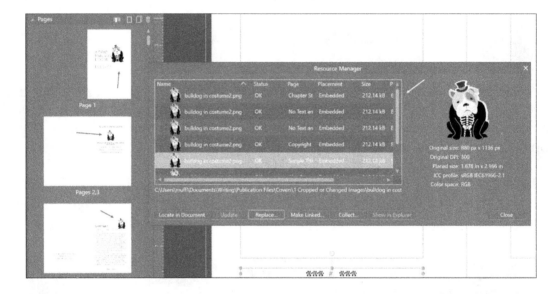

This approach should work as long as you haven't done any fancy work on the image in the Affinity file itself. I recently ran into a situation where it didn't work but I think that was because I'd applied Layer Masks to the image using Affinity Photo.

For what we're doing here though, you should be fine.

So if you set up a template that can work across multiple series with an image as part of the template, then it's only a matter of a minute or two to swap out the image for Series 1 and replace it with the image for Series 2. (Especially if you use images that are the same dimensions so you don't have to click and drag to adjust the images on each of the master pages.)

Now on to the rest of the master pages we want to create. Next up is the Also By page.

ALSO BY PAGE

The next master page we want to create is the Also By page. It looks like this:

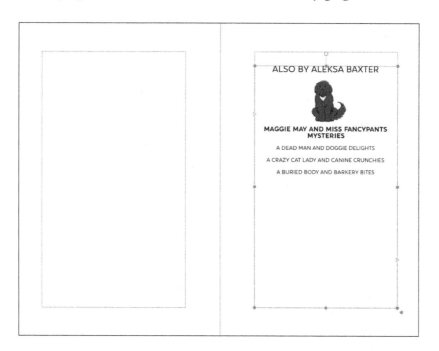

There are three components, a text frame, an image, and text.

You could technically just set up a master page with a blank text box and image and then add your also by text in the Pages section instead, but I prefer to add it here since it's the same across all of the books in the series.

(And if you download one of the templates I've created for others to use you'll see that I've put filler text in this section that can still be edited from the Pages section so I see no reason not to put text on this particular page.)

Okay. First thing we need to do is to create a new master page.

To do that, go to the Master Pages section of the Pages studio and right-click on your existing master page. In the dropdown menu choose Duplicate.

(Insert Master would also work, but it makes for an additional step since we're not changing any of the dimensions or margins compared to our existing master page.)

Duplicate creates an exact copy of the master page you right-clicked on, name and all.

The first thing we want to do is rename the new master page. So scroll down to that newly-created duplicate, click on it, and then click on the name.

The name should now be highlighted in blue.

Type in the name you want (I use Also By) and hit Enter.

Now double-click on the thumbnail image of the master page you just renamed because you want to be sure you're making edits to the right version of the master page. (I can't count the number of times I duplicated a master page, renamed it, and made edits only to realize I'd ended up making those edits to the original and not the copy because I failed to double-click on the correct master page thumbnail.)

Once you've done this, you should have two master pages that are identical in terms of content, but have different names.

Because we copied the title page, we already have a text frame and image in our also by master page. So all we need to do is change the size of the frame, change the size of the image, center and move the image, change the text wrap style, and then add our text.

To change the size of the text frame, go to the Layers studio on the right-hand side and click on the Frame Text layer. This is going to outline that text frame and show the blue circles around the perimeter.

Click and drag the top line of the text frame upward to where you want your also by text to start. My text frame ended up being about six inches tall when I was done because I didn't want the text to start at the top of my text area but I did want it higher than my title page text.

Another option for changing the height of the text frame is to click on it and then use the Transform studio instead. But then you'll have to drag the frame back into place because Affinity adds the height to the bottom not the top.

That's the text frame resized. Next the image.

Click on that layer and this time you can click and drag from the corner at an angle to resize the image while keeping it proportionate.

Your other option is to use the Transform studio. Click on the image, make sure to lock the aspect ratio, and then enter your new value for height or width.

For this page I made the image smaller. It was 2.166 inches high on the title page and here I made it 1.4 inches high.

Once the image is the size you want it, it's time to move and center it. Click on the image and drag it to where you want it to be.

As you drag the image around, you should see green or red lines appear (assuming you've turned on snapping, which you should) as it is centered within one of the pages or frames or aligned with the edge of one of the pages or frames.

What you want is for the image to be centered in your text frame, like it is below, and with enough space above it for there to be a line of 16 point text:

When you center the image, be careful that you are actually aligned to the space you want to be aligned to. Affinity will show when you're centered both on the page and within the text frame. Because print books use a larger interior margin than exterior margin those will not be the same.

So when you move your image around you will see a green line appear indicating the image is centered two separate times. You want the green line that appears when the image is centered in the text frame. You should be able to visually identify this by making sure that the white space on both sides of the image is the same width within that frame as you can see in the screenshot above.

Note that there are alignment options available in the top menu in Affinity, but I prefer to click and drag and use the snapping lines instead for print layouts because of this issue.

(I also might actually move this image off-center if I were trying to create a final book using it, because Affinity is using the frame around the image to center it and as you can see with this image the center of the body of the dog is to the left of the center of the overall image so even though it is technically centered it might not feel that way to a reader.)

Anyway. Place your image where you want it and then it's time to add the text.

Click on the A on the left-hand side and then click into the top of the text box and type the first line of text, in this case "Also By [Author Name]" where [Author Name] is whatever your author name is. Hit Enter.

Format that line with your chosen font and font size. I'm going to use Brushability Sans, Regular, 16 pt. And I want to center this text, which is an option available in the top menu in the center section. Align Center is the second choice.

(It's also available at the top of the Paragraph studio.)

Even though the text will probably look like it's too close to the top of the text frame, it's okay because that text frame line will not exist in the final product. You can see that if you look at the thumbnail of this page on the left under the Master Pages section.

In order to make sure that the next line of text appears below our image instead of across it, we now need to go back to the image and change the text wrap settings.

So click on the image layer (or click on the Move Tool and then the image in the workspace). Next, click on the Show Text Wrap Settings option up top, and then in the Text Wrap dialogue box choose Jump.

Go back to your text tool and click on your text and make sure that the cursor for your second line of text is below the image but that the also by text remains above the image. Like so:

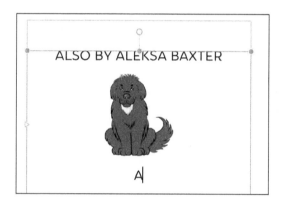

If not, use the Move Tool to move the image until that is the case.

(Because we used Jump for the text wrap setting on that image, the text you add will always be either above or below the image but never on the same line as the image. So you're looking for that sweet spot where the first line of text doesn't have to jump the image, but the second line does.)

Now it's time to add the series title and books for this author. I'm going to type that all in first and then format it.

I want *Maggie May and Miss Fancypants Mysteries* for the series name and then I'm going to list the first three titles in the series, *A Dead Man and Doggie Delights, A Crazy Cat Lady and Canine Crunchies,* and *A Buried Body and Barkery Bites.*

The font will stay the same and the text will stay centered, but I want the series name bolded (Ctrl + B or click on the B in the top menu) and 12 pt. And then the titles regular 10 pt.

For now I'm just going to manually format these lines. Ultimately it's a best practice to have text styles assigned to each of these different lines and I do that in the template, but I don't want to bog us down right this second with learning text styles. So we're going to table that for the time being and just manually format our text.

And that's it. We now have an Also By master page that looks like this:

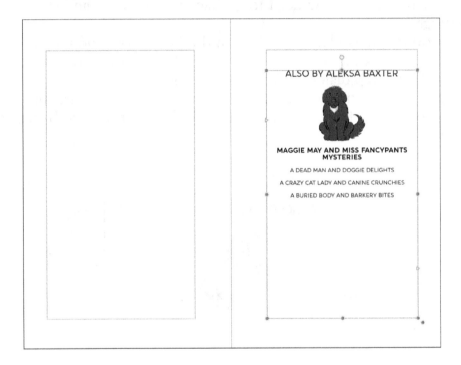

I'd probably tweak that a little more if I was publishing this, but it gives you an idea at least.

ADD ALSO BY MASTER PAGE TO DOCUMENT

We now have two master pages, but in the actual Pages section we still have just the one title page. To add in our also by section, we need to add two pages to our document and then apply the Also By master page to them.

To do that, go to the Pages section, and right-click on the thumbnail for the title page. From the dropdown that appears choose Add Pages.

This will bring up the Add Pages dialogue box. Choose to add 2 pages, After, Page 1, and from the Master Page dropdown menu select the Also By master page.

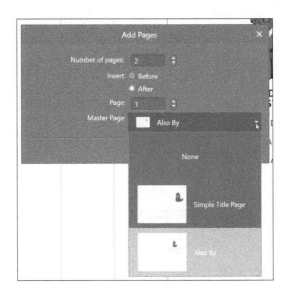

Click OK, and here we go:

Our document, which is what's shown in the Pages section, now has a title page as well as the two-page Also By spread.

You can edit the text on the Also By page in the Pages section or in the Master Pages section. But if there's ever a typo or another permanent fix you need to make, it's best to fix it in the Master Pages section. This is because of how changes made in one section impact the other.

Changes made in the Pages section will not carry back to the Master Pages section.

But changes made in the Master Pages section will carry forward to every *new* use of that master page in the Pages section. If you've already edited a two-page spread in the Pages section, new changes to that master page in the Master Pages section will *not* carry forward to that page. If you haven't made any edits in the Pages section, though, they will.

(This is my conclusion based on trial and error. I know that sounds a little confusing, but basically if you make changes for the series or the template in the master pages and make changes for that specific title in the Pages section, you're probably going to be fine. Worst-case scenario, if the changes you make on a master page don't carry through to the Pages section and you need them to, then delete that page spread in the Pages section and add it again and they should.)

Okay. Next up is the copyright and chapter start master page.

COPYRIGHT AND CHAPTER START
MASTER PAGE

The copyright and chapter start master page is a little more complex because we're going to have text frames on both pages this time as well as adding a footer. What we want to end up with is this:

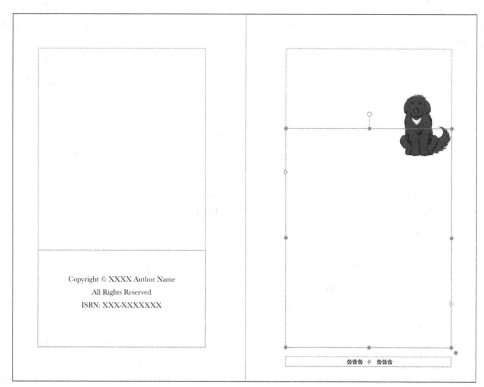

First step, go to the Master Pages section of the Pages studio and Duplicate the Title Page to create a new master page. Rename it Copyright and Chapter Start.

Left-click on that thumbnail in the Master Pages section and drag the master page to the end. You should see a blue line appear after the Also By master page, release when that happens and the Copyright master page should move to the bottom of the list of master pages.

(Note that you can minimize the Pages section if you want to by clicking on the little arrow next to Pages. That will let you see all of your master pages at once.)

Double-click on the thumbnail for the copyright master page to make sure it's the master page that's shown in your main workspace.

Now add a text frame on the left-hand side of the master page. (Frame Text Tool, click and drag. Align along the edges with the red and green lines.)

How big this text frame should be will depend on how much copyright language you want to include. I do the bare bones—just author name, all rights reserved, and the ISBN—so my text frame is small and at the bottom of the text area. If you did one more like a traditional publisher your text frame might need to be the entire text area.

Once you have the text frame, click on the Artistic Text Tool option (the A) on the left-hand side set of options, click into the text frame, and add your text. Format the text in your desired font.

I use 12 pt Baskerville URW centered. This is the same font and font size I will use for the main body text. You will likely not have that font available, but Garamond is a good choice and one you should have by default.

I highly recommend with any fiction title that you focus on one accent font for your chapter headers, book title page, etc. and one font for your main body text, copyright information, headers and footers, etc. So here I'm using Brushability Sans and Baskerville URW.

The font you choose for your chapter headers and title page can be more ornate or playful because it's only used as an accent. Ideally it should have multiple weights available and be a sans serif font, a decorative font, or a script font.

Brushability Sans is a sans serif font and has five different weights (Light, Regular, Semibold, Bold, and Black) available. The different weights give me a nice variety of choices for my different pages without requiring that I add a third font to my book. And the fact that it's a sans serif font keeps it from conflicting with my main body text which is a serifed font.

For your main body text you want a workhorse font that is easy to read. Unless you're doing large print or publishing for a specific audience with reading impairments, the font should be a serifed font because that's easier to read for most people. All of the Amazon templates use Garamond. Other good choices per IngramSpark are Caslon, Minion, and Palatino. Whatever font you choose, be sure you also have the italic version available because in Affinity you can only add italics if you have the italic version of a font.

If you have a book where you really loved the fonts sometimes they'll include a page at the back of the book that names the font.

You should be able to just type a c in parens—(c)—and it will automatically convert to the copyright symbol for you, but it doesn't work for me all of the time. (As I've been writing this book it's failed to work about 60% of the time, but has worked about 40% of the time.)

If it doesn't work for you, click where you want that symbol and then go to View-> Studio-> Glyph Browser to open the glyph browser studio.

If you've already applied your font that should be the font shown at the top. If it isn't, use the dropdown menu to choose the font you're going to use and then scroll down through the section that shows all of the letters and symbols in that font until you see the copyright symbol.

Double-click on it to add it to your document. It should appear at the point where you'd clicked into your document.

Once you've done that the first time the symbol should also be listed at the bottom of the glyph browser in your most recently used symbols section. You can double-click it from there as well.

Okay. Getting back to our master page. I entered and formatted my text and here's what I ended up with:

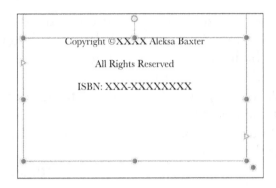

The X's are there to remind me that for each actual title I create I need to add the copyright year and ISBN.

Now, in the screenshot above that's the default spacing, but I want my lines of text to be closer together.

To fix that, I select the text, and go to the Paragraph studio in the top right of the workspace, click the checkbox for Space Between Same Styles, and then change the value there to 6 pt.

That brings each line of text closer together but not so close they're squished. I also want to change the size of that text frame to bring this text a little lower down on the page. I end up with this (keeping in mind that that line right above Copyright will not be visible on the page when I print this):

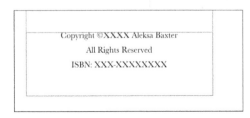

Next we need to put our chapter start on the right-hand side of the page.

In general, chapters in fiction books do not start at the top of the page. They usually start a certain amount of space lower. It'll be up to you where you want to set yours based on what "looks good", just be sure that it's enough space down the page to be a clear difference from being at the top of the page.

Also, keeping in mind that both your chapter headers (Chapter 1, Chapter 2, etc.) as well as your main body text will be in this text frame.

DO NOT try creating a separate text box for your chapter header, not unless you want to complicate your life in horrible ways. (Ask me how I know…)

I'm going to leave this one at a height of 4.75 which matches the title page. It'll create a smoother line for someone flipping through the book for those to be at the same height. That means I don't have to do anything to the text frame because it's already good to go.

Now that that's set, we're going to include our little dog image on the right-hand side and top of the text box. (You do not have to do this and for some it may seem like overkill to have an image at every chapter start, but just to show you what you could do with your chapter starts I'm going to do so.)

The image is already there, but I want to resize it because I want it a little smaller than it is on the title page.

Again, for consistency across pages, I'll use the same size as I did on the Also By page which was a height of 1.4. So I use the Transform studio to change the size of the image, making sure that the Lock Aspect Ratio option is checked.

I can then click and drag the image until it's aligned to the right-hand side of my text frame and centered along the top edge of the text frame for my chapter start. (I may decide to adjust that later if it doesn't look right with text added, but it's a good place to start.)

Finally, we need to add our footer to the bottom of the page.

Click on the Frame Text Tool (T) option and then click and drag to make a text frame that's located a little bit below the main text area. You want a text frame that is as wide as your main text frame and a little taller than the height of one line of the font that you're going to use in the main body of your document. (See the screenshot above for what I did.)

Next, click on the A, Artistic Text Tool, and click back into that text frame. Go to Text-> Insert -> Fields -> Page Number to insert a page number.

You should now see a # sign in that text frame. (In your actual document that will display as a number but in the master page it shows as a # sign.) Format it with the same font and font size as your main body text and center it.

(You can also choose to align away from spine instead of centering if you want, but I'm going to center. If you choose to align away from spine that will put your page numbers on the outer edge of each page. That option is available using the dropdown arrow at the end of the alignment options or at the top of the Paragraph studio.)

I also make sure to center the text in my footers vertically as well. To do that, use the top menu option to the right of where you center your text. It's a dropdown menu that is by default Top Aligned.

The reason I do that is because I had a book where I didn't do that and the book used images and for some reason that changed the alignment of my page numbers at the bottom of the page so that the page numbers where there were images on the page were lower than the page numbers where there weren't images.

If you want, you can also add images or flourishes around the page number as well.

Based on my experience, adding little flourishes that you can get from one of the fonts in the glyph browser is much easier than adding actual images to the document, but both are possible.

For this series I use a font called Ennobled Pet to put some paw prints on either side of my page number. I put three asterisks on either side and assign that font to it.

And here we are, a complete Copyright and Chapter Start page:

TEXT AND CHAPTER START MASTER PAGE

We're going to let that one sit for a minute while we create a couple more master pages.

Next one up is the Text and Chapter Start master page, which looks like this:

The easiest way to do this is to copy the Copyright and Chapter Start master page and then modify it.

So. Right-click, Duplicate, and then rename the new one. Double-click on the new one to make sure you're editing the right version.

The right-hand side of the master page is already done.

The first thing we need to do on the left-hand side is expand the text frame to fit the entire text space and then delete the copyright text. So, click on the text frame, use the blue circle to drag it to the top, then select the text in the frame and delete it.

Next, we need to add a header and footer to this page.

The footer is easy enough, you can just copy the footer from the right-hand page and drag that copy into place on the left-hand page.

You can do this a few ways. The first option is to go to the Layers studio, find the page number layer, right-click, Duplicate, then go to the workspace and click on the page number layer and drag it to the left.

A second option is to click on the Move Tool and then click on the footer in the workspace, Ctrl + C and then Ctrl+ V to copy and paste, and then left-click and drag the copy to its new location on the left-hand page.

With both options, make sure that when you click and drag your new footer aligns with the old footer as well as the text area on the left-hand page. Like so:

If for some reason the snapping lines aren't appearing, try clicking on your footer layers in the Layers panel first. Or you can just take the Y value from the Transform studio for the original footer and use the same Y value for the new one.

Now we need our header. Copy the footer and move it to the top.

It's easy enough to align it with your active text space but a little trickier to place it at the same distance from the main text frame as you placed your footer. To do that, click on the footer and arrow up and then down to see the numeric value that is shown next to the blue arrowed line drawn between the main text frame and the footer text frame.

You can then click on the header text frame and arrow up or down until you get the same value between the header text frame and main text frame. In my case I was able to get within .01 of the same value which should be visually about the same to a reader.

After the header is in place, you need to delete the text that's currently in there and then replace it with the header information. In fiction books you generally have the author name on the left-hand page and the book title on the right-hand page. Affinity lets you use fields to add both of these, but we need to set those field values up first for it to work.

To do so, go to the Fields studio which should be on the right-hand top side. Click into the space next to Author and add your author name. And then click into the space next to Title and add your book title.

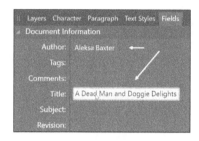

Now click into the header text frame, delete the text that's there, and add your Author field.

To do that, go to the Fields studio and double-click on Author on the left-hand side. (So not the Author Name you typed in on the right-hand side, but the label.) This will insert the *value* you have listed for Author into that text frame, not the field name.

(If you used a special font to add accents to your footers like I had, you may then need to change the font to your chosen main body font.)

If the Fields studio isn't open or you can't find it, you can go to Text-> Insert-> Fields and then choose More from the dropdown. That will open the Fields studio for you.

And that's it. There you have it. A master page for when there's text on the left-hand side of the page and a chapter start on the right-hand side of the page.

Okay, now the Text and Text master page and then we can start creating the beginning of our book.

TEXT AND TEXT MASTER PAGE

The Text and Text master page is for those portions of the book where there's just text on both sides of the page. It looks like this:

To create the Text and Text master page, duplicate the Text and Chapter Start master page you just created and rename it. Be sure to double-click on the renamed master page so that you're editing the right one. (I say this multiple times because it's a mistake I make often and then I have to change the names around.)

Okay. We already have the left-hand side done. We just need to fix the right-hand side.

So. Delete the image. Be sure you have the Move Tool selected if you want to click on the image in the workspace itself, otherwise go to the Layers studio and click on the layer with the image in it and then hit the Delete key.

Next, resize the text box for that side so that it covers the entire text area.

After that, copy the header from the left-hand page over to the right-hand page. You can do that in the Layers panel or right-click, Copy, Paste in the workspace itself. Click and drag so that your header on your right-hand page is aligned with your header on the left-hand page as well as the text area for the right-hand page.

Now click on the A for the Artistic Text Tool. Go back to that header on the right-hand page and delete the Author name. Replace it with the field for Title by going to the Fields studio and double-clicking on Title. Note that Affinity will insert your value for that field not the field name.

You should now have a master page spread with your author name in the header on the left, your title in the header on the right, page numbers in the footers, and two text frames that are the size of the designated text area:

Done.

BUILD THE BEGINNING OF YOUR DOCUMENT

So far your actual document has a title page and an also by page. We now need to add two more page spreads to that document. To do so, go to the Pages section. (If you minimized it, it will be at the bottom of the Pages studio.)

Click on the also by page spreads, Pages 2, 3. Right-click. Choose Add Pages from the dropdown.

In the Add Pages dialogue box you want 2 pages, After, Page 3, and Copyright and Chapter Start for the master page. OK.

Next, right-click on that newly-added page spread, Pages 4, 5, which should be the Copyright and Chapter Start pages, and choose Add Pages again.

This time it's 2 pages, After, Page 5, and the dropdown option you want is Text and Text.

That should give you a document with seven pages.

The first is your title page, followed by a blank page and Also By, followed by a copyright page and your first chapter start, followed by two pages for just text that have a header and footer.

It should look like the screenshot on the next page.

Alright, now that that's done, we're almost ready to add our main document text, but one thing we haven't addressed yet is text flow between frames. Let's do that next.

TEXT FLOW BETWEEN FRAMES

One of the wonders of Affinity (or probably any professional print design program) is that you can have your text flow from one text frame to the next automatically. The key though is that you have to link them so that Affinity knows you want that to happen.

To do so, go to the Master Pages section and open the Text and Text master page by double-clicking on it.

You should have two text frames, one on each page. The problem is, we haven't linked them yet. So any text I paste into that left-hand text frame will stay in that left-hand text frame. And any text I paste into that right-hand text frame will stay in that right-hand text frame.

But what I want is for the text in the left-hand frame to flow to the right-hand frame once the left-hand frame fills up.

To make that happen, we need to tell Affinity to continue any additional text from the left-hand main text frame into the right-hand main text frame.

It's very easy to do.

First, click on the text frame on the left-hand side. When you do this, you should see that the text frame has an outline and that there are little blue arrows visible on the left and right edges of the text frame.

Click on the blue arrow on the right-hand edge of that left-hand text frame and then click into the text frame on the right-hand page. Before your click on the right-hand text frame it will be shaded in blue like this to show you where the text will flow to:

After you click on that right-hand text frame that will disappear, but you should now see a line that connects the two text frames.

That line tells you that when there is too much text to fit in the left-hand frame, it will flow to the right-hand frame. It will *follow* that line in the direction of that arrow. (This is important to keep in mind in case you ever get that reversed. I once tried to create a master page by copying an existing master page and swapping the text frames that were already linked and it reversed the flow of the text so that it went right-to-left. So the direction of those arrows matters.)

For each master page that you create that has more than one main text frame you need to tell Affinity to flow the text between the frames. That means right now we also need to do this for the Text and Chapter Start master page. Go and do that. It's the same process. Click on the blue arrow on the right edge of the left-hand text frame and then click on the right-hand text frame.

(I probably should have had you do it when we created the templates, but this is the order in which my mind thinks of these things and as long as you get them all into place by the end, you're fine.)

That's text flow between text frames within master pages, but we also need to tell Affinity to flow text between our two main body master pages that we just added, pages 4, 5 and 6, 7 in the Pages section.

To do so, double-click on the Pages 4, 5 thumbnail in the Pages section. Then in the main workspace scroll down a bit until you can see the bottom of Pages 4, 5 and the top of Pages 6, 7.

Now, click on the text frame on the right-hand page for Pages 4, 5 (the top of the two spreads that you can see). Then click on that blue arrow on the right edge of the frame. Next, click on the main text frame on the left-hand side for Pages 6, 7 (the bottom of the two spreads that you can see). It should look like this when you're done, with a blue line connecting Page 5 to Page 6:

This tells Affinity to take text from that chapter start master page and flow it down to the text and text master page that comes next.

Okay. We basically have everything in place at the moment to bring in our main document text. Once we do that, we'll talk about text styles.

It doesn't feel like it, but with this groundwork we've laid we are probably 75% of the way there right now because Affinity is about to do a lot of the heavy lifting for us.

ADD YOUR MAIN BODY TEXT

At this point you're going to ignore the Master Pages section of the Pages studio for the time being. Minimize it. Put it away. Click on that little arrow next to Master Pages and let's focus in on our Pages section and the document we want to create.

(We will be going back to it later because there are more master pages we still need to create, but for now let's move on to something more interesting.)

Okay. Double-click on the thumbnail for the pages that have your first chapter start. For me that's pages 4, 5. You should now see both of those pages in your main workspace.

If for some reason you can't easily see both pages in your view, go to View-> Zoom and then Zoom to Fit or Zoom to Width. One of those two should work so that you can see both pages of the spread in your workspace at the same time. Usually I run into this visibility issue when I move from the Master Page section to the Pages section, I don't know why.

Now, go to wherever you have the main body text of your document stored and copy that text. You don't want your front matter or back matter, but you do want all of the chapters. All of them. Chapter headers and text.

So, Ctrl + A to select all, Ctrl + C to copy, at least in Word.

Next, click into the main text frame where your first chapter is supposed to start and use Ctrl + V to paste your text.

If you can't click into the text box, be sure you've clicked on the A on the left-hand side first to activate the Artistic Text Tool.

You should see something like this.

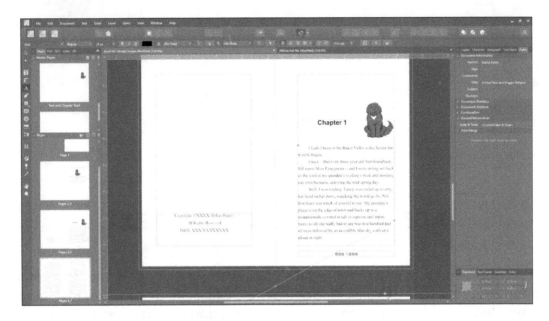

Because we already told Affinity to flow the text from this page to the next, it does. We have three pages of text and the beginning of a novel.

But you can't see more text than that even though we pasted in more than a hundred pages of text because there are no more pages for the text to flow to. It's in the document right now, just not visible.

And you can tell that there's more text hiding, because on the right-edge of that chapter start page and where there's normally a blue circle, it's now red. Scroll down to the next two pages and you'll see more red circles and possibly a red arrow on the right-hand edge of the last main text frame there on page 7.

That's because we pasted in more text than there was space for and those red marks are Affinity telling you that.

This is a key thing to understand about Affinity if you're used to working in Word like I am. Because in Word you usually see all of your text. But in Affinity you can have text that isn't visible because Affinity will only display text in your text frames and if there aren't enough of them it just doesn't display that text. But the text is still there.

I'm hitting on this one hard, because I get caught out by this on a somewhat regular basis.

For example, I will delete all of the pages of a two hundred page document and think that's all I needed to do because I no longer see that text. But behind the scenes Affinity still has the text that was in those two hundred pages.

So I always have to remind myself to delete the text first. And then I can delete the pages, too.

Sometimes this pops up when I go to create a table of contents and it puts in an about the author section, for example, that I didn't realize was still there. So if that ever happens to you, that's why.

Okay. Putting that aside, right now we have three pages of our main document and about two hundred pages of text that's there but you can't see.

It's time to tell Affinity to add enough pages and flow that remaining text to make it all visible.

To do this, go to the right-hand main text frame of the Text and Text page spread on pages 6,7, so the frame on page 7.

If you see a red circle along the right-hand edge, click on it. It should turn into a red arrow. Otherwise you should see the red arrow and a little eye with a slash through it that looks like this:

> With a shotgun.
>
> There I was, hanging onto the fence, Fancy barking her head off at my feet, and my grandpa comes walking around the side of the house to confront the guy, shotgun in hand. At least I was pretty sure it was a

What you want to do is hold down the Shift key and click on that red arrow on the right-hand edge of the right-most text frame.

If you do this right, Affinity should start adding pages for you and flowing your text to those new pages.

The reason I had you add a Text and Text master page as the last page spread in our document is because Affinity adds pages using whatever master page spread you were using on that last page. Since the bulk of the pages in a novel are text and text, having Affinity use that master page spread to add our pages saves us the most effort because it's already applying our most frequently-used master page spread for us.

So here we go. With just that shift and click I suddenly have a document with 239 pages of text all placed neatly in my text frames and flowing from one page to the next.

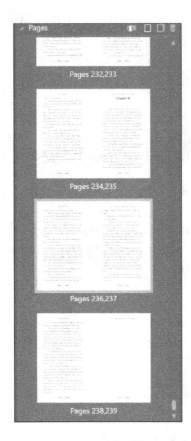

Isn't that awesome? Think how much time and energy that just saved us. No inserting master pages, no linking text frames. All of it already done for us.

Okay. Now we need to put in place our text styles to save even more time and energy.

TEXT STYLES

A text style is a shortcut that allows you to apply formatting to your text in a quick and easy way. Once you set up one you never have to go through the process of choosing your font, font weight, font size, paragraph and character formatting, etc. again to get that specific appearance. You can just apply the text style.

Even better, you can assign keyboard shortcuts to your text styles which can save a ton of time when formatting the main body of your document. I usually have text styles and shortcuts assigned to my chapter headers, my first paragraph, and my main body text. That lets me quickly move through my entire document and apply formatting to the text as needed.

Sometimes for non-fiction I also have a text style and shortcut assigned to subheaders as well.

FIRST PARAGRAPH TEXT STYLE

Okay. So how do we set a text style up?

It's pretty easy. We'll start with the first paragraph text style.

Go to your first page of the main body of your document. This is Chapter 1 for most of us and should be Page 5 if you've been following along and building a document according to what I've listed out here.

Click on the Artistic Text Tool and then highlight your first paragraph.

Now choose all of the formatting you want for that paragraph from the top menu options. For me that's going to be Baskerville URW, Regular, 12 pt, Align Left.

(In the actual books I've published for this series I used Justify Left instead. Those are the two common choices you have for paragraph formatting.)

Next, go to the Paragraph studio and set your Leading to the desired value. I usually use Default which in this case shows as 14.4. And because this is a first paragraph and I don't want it indented, I also need to go to the second option on the left-hand side of the Spacing section and set the First Line Indent value to 0.

Once the paragraph looks the way you want it to, it's time to save this formatting as a Text Style.

In the top menu next to the Paragraph mark, you should see a dropdown that currently reads [No Style]. Be careful, because there may be two of them and you want the second one. Click on that dropdown arrow and the second option should be New Style.

Click on that. This will open the Create Paragraph Style dialogue box which looks like this:

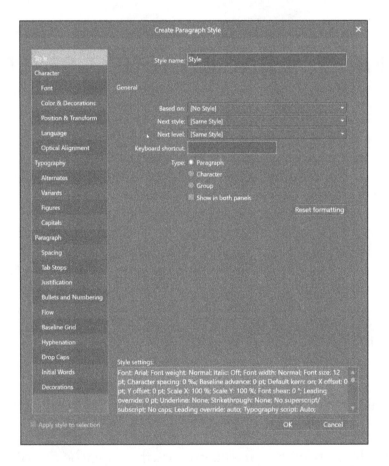

If there aren't that many options on the left-hand side, you probably went to the wrong dropdown and opened the Create Character Style dialogue box instead. If so, close and use the other dropdown menu.

First things first, in the Style Name box, type in the name you want to use for this style. Make it something descriptive that you can immediately identify. I like to use First Paragraph for my first paragraph style.

At this point, because we already formatted the paragraph in our document, it's ready to go and we could just click on OK and be done right now. But while we're here, let's add a keyboard shortcut for this one.

I like to use Shift + 1 for Chapter Heading, Shift + 2 for First Paragraph, and Shift + 3 for Main Body text. Having them in order like that makes it easy for me to just go through in my head which one I need. (I sometimes use the wrong one still as you'll see in the videos, but that's an easy enough fix.) And they are also easy to reach when I'm typing.

I don't necessarily recommend using the same shortcut keys I do. Because if you think about it for a second, you'll realize that those are also the exclamation mark, at sign, and pound sign. For me it works because what I'm doing in Affinity is 99% formatting. If I were also typing a lot of text in Affinity I'd run into an issue where instead of, for example, getting an exclamation mark as planned, I reformatted a paragraph.

It doesn't happen to me often enough for me to change that up, although I do run into this problem with my books on Excel where I use Shift + 4 for subheaders and also need to make a few edits that involve the $ sign.

Okay. So pick the key combination you want for your keyboard shortcut for your first paragraph. Mine is going to be Shift + 2.

Go to the Keyboard Shortcut field and type the shortcut. So, for me, I'd hold down the Shift key and type 2. Affinity will interpret what you type and place a description of what you typed into the text box for you.

Once that's done you can click on OK and you have a First Paragraph text style that can be applied using your keyboard shortcut.

MAIN BODY TEXT STYLE

In an ideal world, your text styles would be nested, meaning that you have one primary text style that uses your main body font and you have another primary text style that uses your accent font. Any other text styles that use those same fonts would be secondary to the primary text styles. This way, if you wanted to change your font from say, Baskerville URW to Garamond, you could do so by editing just one text style.

Sounds confusing, I know. But in execution it's much easier. So let's do that now with our main body text.

What I want you to do is go to the second paragraph in that first chapter, which should be your first main body paragraph. And I want you to apply the first paragraph text style to it. So Shift + 2 for me.

If you didn't have a keyboard shortcut set up you could choose the style from the dropdown menu in the top section or you could go to the Text Styles studio and choose it from there.

Now that we have this paragraph formatted as a First Paragraph we can edit it to be a main body paragraph. The only difference for me between the first paragraph and the main body paragraph is the paragraph indent.

So I go to the Paragraph studio, go to the Spacing section, and change the value for the second option on the left-hand side (First Line Indent) to .2.

My paragraph is no longer using the First Paragraph style. And if you look at the dropdown menu up top for text style you will see that it shows as First Paragraph+. That is telling you that you started with the First Paragraph text style, but have made edits to it.

If you are ever trying to update a text style and want that text style to now use your updates, you can do so by clicking on the paragraph mark with a swoosh to the right of that dropdown menu.

It will only be an available option if you have in some way changed the formatting of that paragraph. But that is NOT what we want right now. We want to create a new style based on the old one.

So click on the dropdown arrow next to the style name, go to the top of the dropdown using the bar on the right-hand side, and choose New Style again.

This will open the Create Paragraph Style dialogue box once more.

Type in the name you want for the style in the Style Name box. I'm going to use Body Text. Also add your keyboard shortcut. I'm using Shift + 3.

And note what it looks like at the bottom for the style settings description.

It's basically saying, "Whatever that first paragraph does, do that, and then indent the line by this much."

Which is great when you want to change out the font or the font size for the entire novel. Right? You just update the First Paragraph style and this one will update as well.

That can also be dangerous, though, if you forget that you have your styles linked in this way and you try changing one style and forget that it will impact all of the others.

So you need to give a little thought to which of your styles you use for that primary style.

I have in the past (because I do make all the mistakes at some point in time) made a header and footer style my primary and linked a section header style as secondary and then forgotten. When I did it they were both centered and that was fine. But then I changed the header and footer style to be aligned to outer edge of the page and that automatically changed the section header to be the same, which did not work.

Just be careful and think it through. And be sure that your last step with any book you format is to look through the entire book, page by page, and make sure that everything looks good.

Click OK and you have your second style. We just need one more for our chapter headings.

CHAPTER HEADING TEXT STYLE

Highlight your first chapter heading or title. For me that's Chapter 1.

Now apply the formatting you want for that heading.

I'm going to stick with Brushability Sans, in a SemiBold weight and 20 pt size. I want it left-aligned because I have that image there on the right-hand side.

I also want some space before the first line of text.

If you are ever tempted to create distance between lines of text using an Enter, stop. There is a paragraph formatting option that will do that for you and will always keep things consistent. You do not want extra Enters anywhere in your document. What you want is to add a value for Space After Paragraph. In this case, 12 pt. It's found in the Paragraph studio on the right-hand side of the Spacing section.

Once your formatting is set, go to the dropdown, click on New Style, name your style, assign your keyboard shortcut (mine for this is Shift + 1), and click OK.

This style is one that should not be based on your first paragraph or body text styles because it uses the accent font, but it can be a good one to base all of your front matter styles off of if you want to create styles for those.

APPLY MAIN BODY
TEXT STYLE TO ALL

We now have the three primary text styles that we need for the main body of the book.

If we had also used styles in Word or wherever we copied our text from and Affinity had carried over those style names (which it does sometimes) we could now do a find and replace for each paragraph style and be done with assigning those text styles.

But since I used an RTF file from Vellum which does not carry over, I now have to apply those styles manually.

Since body text is going to be the majority of the text in this book, I use Ctrl + A to select all of the text I pasted into the main body and then Shift + 3 to apply the Body Text style format to everything. (It won't impact my front matter, because those pages are not linked to these text frames.)

By doing that I did erase the pretty formatting I put in place for my chapter start and my first paragraph, but that's easy enough to solve. I click on the line with Chapter 1 and use Shift + 1 and then I click on the line below that for my first paragraph and use Shift +2. And this is what I have for the first page:

CHAPTER 1

I hadn't been in the Baker Valley a day before the trouble began.

Fancy—that's my three-year-old Newfoundland, full name Miss Fancypants—and I were sitting out back in the yard at my grandpa's reading a book and minding our own business, enjoying the mid-spring day.

Well, I was reading. Fancy was curled up nearby, her head on her paws, watching the world go by. Not that there was much of a world to see. My grandpa's place is on the edge of town and backs up to a mountainside covered in tall evergreens and aspen trees, so all she really had to see was five hundred feet of trees followed by an incredibly blue sky without a cloud in sight.

Man, I love Colorado.

Anyway. There we were, minding our own business, not bothering a soul, when Fancy jumped up and raced to the fence, barking like a mad woman. And it wasn't her "Hey, is that a dog, can we play?" bark either. It was her, "There's a jerk too close to my home" bark.

I reluctantly set my book aside—I'd just gotten to the good part, too—and dragged myself over to see what

It looks like it should in terms of paragraph and chapter heading formats.

ASSESS YOUR APPEARANCE

Now that you've created a first chapter master page and dropped in your text, it's time to stop and assess your document's appearance.

Look at that first page.

Does it look good to you?

Do you like where the image is relative to the text and chapter header? Do you like the amount of space between the chapter header and the first line of text? Do you like the fonts you're using? Do you like where the chapter starts on the page? Should it be higher? Should it be lower?

What about the justification you're using? Do you like having a ragged right margin if that's what you have? Do you like having the paragraphs justified if that's what you went with? Should you hyphenate your words to make it look better?

(To change justification go to the top menu or the Paragraph studio. To add hyphenation go to the Paragraph studio, Hyphenation section, and click Use Auto-Hyphenation.)

What about line spacing? Is there enough space between lines but not too much? What about the main body indent? Did you indent enough but not too much?

Basically, is this how you want your book to look?

Because if you change your mind later it's going to be a lot of redone work to go back and do the next steps again. So right now is the time to make these decisions. If that image needs to move, go fix it on the master page right now. If that chapter header needs to be bigger or smaller or have a bigger space from the text, fix it now.

Anything that's nagging at you, fix.

For example, I think I want that image to be up a bit, more in line with my chapter header than centered on that line. So I'm going to make that change in the two master pages I have that contain that image right now.

If you do move that image, use the Transform studio to make sure that the image is at the same height (Y) on both pages.

Yep. I like this much better.

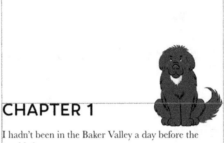

By fixing this now I avoid a lot of extra, unnecessary work. Normally I'd probably justify my paragraphs as well, but I'm going to leave them as is.

* * *

There's also one other choice you need to make that you can't see so much right now. That's how to handle widows and orphans. These are single lines that appear at the top or bottom of the page that are part of a paragraph but have been separated from it. You're really not supposed to have them if you can avoid it.

Now is the time to decide whether you want Affinity to automatically remove them for you, which may result in the text on facing pages ending at different points on the page, or whether you'll try to fix them manually. I fix mine by hand because I like my text to line up at the bottom of the page.

If you want Affinity to do that for you (and I do have Affinity do it for large print where that matters more), then go to the Paragraph studio, Flow Options section, and check the boxes to prevent them.

* * *

Finalize your overall appearance now. Because from here on out we are going to be fixing little fiddly issues and assigning master pages based upon where your text falls on the page and that is driven by all of these decisions.

SECTION BREAKS

Next up, it's time to figure out what you want to do about section breaks, because in a lot of instances you can handle them all at once with a find and replace.

I once made the mistake of using an image for a section break and that was time-consuming and annoying because I had issues getting it to center for me which meant I had to place each one individually and click and drag it around to get it where I needed it.

Ever since then I've stuck to fonts or glyphs that are available in my glyph browser.

For example, for my cozy mysteries I use the Ennobled Pet font. It turns an asterisk into a cute little dog paw print.

The full formatting I use is that font, 12 pt, with 6 pt spacing above and below, and centered. Because I'm basically using * * * as my section divider and I don't use that anywhere else, I can easily do a find and replace throughout the whole document and update my section breaks all at once.

(I do need to keep in mind when I do this that I still want to apply the first paragraph text style to each paragraph that follows a section break, but at least it saves a little effort.)

And don't think that there aren't some good possibilities using text only. For example in my fantasy series I was able to use moons and stars for the section breaks because one of the Wingdings fonts includes them. I also have fonts I've bought that come with a separate embellishment version that has all sorts of little lines and shapes to use. So you can still get creative with your section breaks without that much effort.

So how do we apply a style to all of our breaks at once?

You're going to use the Find and Replace studio. If you set your workspace up like mine it will be the second tab on the left-hand side. Find pretty much works like in any standard program. Type your text in below where it says Find and then click on the Find option to show your results.

It will give a listing of all results for that symbol, word, or phrase. Click on each one to go to that page in your document.

So in this case, I would search for * * *, click on Find, and then click on the first result it gave me.

In my workspace, that section break is now highlighted and I can format it however I want and then create a new text style for it. I'm going to creatively name mine Section Break.

Once you've done that, you can go back to the Find and Replace studio and in the Replace section add the text you used for your revised section break (for me that's still * * *) and then click on the little gear symbol off to the right-hand side, go down to Paragraph Style, and choose your Section Break paragraph style.

(I will note here that there have been times when I tried to search for a style that should have been there in that list and it wasn't. So this isn't 100% but it works most of the time.)

You should now see your paragraph style name directly below the replace field. Like this:

Once you have everything set, click on Replace All and Affinity will replace all of your initial section breaks with the new one formatted the way you wanted using your section break style.

You should then be able to click on the search results to navigate through the document and see that all of your section breaks are now formatted the way you wanted. If you really want to, you can update each paragraph after your breaks to use the first paragraph style as you do so. (I am generally not that efficient, but it would be a smart thing to do.)

FIND AND REPLACE
FOR CHAPTER HEADINGS

If you really wanted to get fancy with saving time, you could also use find and replace for your chapter headings, assuming they are listed as Chapter 1, Chapter 2, etc.

Because the text style we assigned to chapter headings is for the whole "paragraph" you can do a find and replace for the word Chapter that replaces it with the word Chapter and assigns the Chapter Header text style.

If you do that, the whole line will be assigned that text style. So even though you only searched for Chapter and not Chapter 1, both words will get the new format.

Obviously this doesn't work if you just used numbers and not the word "chapter." It also doesn't work if you name your chapters.

And keep in mind that any paragraph that includes the word "chapter" is going to get that formatting as well and you'll have to fix it.

I don't normally do this, but it could save time if you wanted to.

THE MAIN BODY OF YOUR DOCUMENT

Now that everything looks the way you want it to, you're ready to start walking through the document and applying master pages, text styles, and fixing any issues with your text such as orphans, widows, too short a word ending a paragraph, a chapter ending with a single line or two on a page, and any other errors or issues that look "wrong".

To do this, start at your first page and work your way forward. You have to do this in order because every fix you apply to an earlier page can impact the fix you need to apply to a later page.

For example, if I apply a chapter start master page that pushes the text on that page down to account for where the chapter heading starts and to make room for the chapter heading, that then impacts which lines of text are at the top and bottom of the next page.

So I don't want to fix an orphan on page 25 if I haven't assigned the chapter start master page on page 20. That orphan may no longer exist once the appropriate master pages have been applied.

And I don't want to apply a master page for a chapter start on page 100 if I haven't fixed a prior chapter that ends with just one line of text on the page, because once I do that, page 100 will no longer be where that chapter starts.

You have to work your way through from the first page to the last. And if you make any big universal formatting changes (like your font, font size, line spacing, etc.) then you have to go back to that first page and start again. That's why we did that assessment earlier. Because you don't want to have to redo all this work. So get it right before you start.

Now let's walk through everything you're going to do.

APPLY TEXT STYLES

Applying text styles is easy if you set it up like I did.

For each chapter start, Shift + 1. For each first paragraph of a chapter or section, Shift + 2. And you shouldn't actually have to use Shift + 3 because we already formatted all of our text with it. But just in case, it's there to use. (For example, if you used find and replace for chapter headings and it turns out you had a paragraph that contained the word chapter.)

Applying master pages, takes a little more effort. Let's talk about that next.

APPLY MASTER PAGES

Here I have the start of Chapter 2. It's nice and easy to see because the text from Chapter 1 ends fairly high up on the prior page.

complications that might delay the opening that that was Jamie-speak for all hell had broken loose. I needed to see just how bad things were.

As I pulled out of the driveway I figured at least it wasn't going to be worse than my grandpa pointing a shotgun at someone, right?

Wrong.

Chapter 2

By the time I reached the store I'd calmed down enough to see the humor in the whole shotgun situation. It helped that I had a good twenty minute drive to get there. And not through urban sprawl like I was used to, but along a two-lane highway that wound its way through cattle land that was green with spring and dotted with the occasional red barn or one-story ranch home tucked away half a mile off the highway, usually down some rutted dirt road separated from the rest of the world by a rusted metal gate.

The whole area is called Baker Valley because it's a long narrow valley tucked into the Colorado mountains. For tourist trap purposes the towns in the area all agreed to pool their advertising funds and advertise the whole valley, but there are actually a half dozen small towns spread throughout the area. My grandpa's place is at the west end of the valley in a town creatively named Creek that has two gas stations, one church, the county seat, a funeral home, a pioneer museum, and about forty houses, half of which probably started off as mobile homes until someone built a foundation around them.

About ten minutes from there is the town of Masonville. It's where everyone in the valley goes to school and boasts its own McDonald's and a supermarket. (New additions in the last decade. Prior to that folks would drive the hour and half into Denver to stock up on groceries once a month, assuming they didn't live on the deer they hunted and the vegetables they grew in their backyard.)

Another ten minutes past Masonville is the shining

Because this is the beginning of Chapter 2, I need a different master page than Text and Text. I need the Text and Chapter Start master page here.

The way to do that is to find the thumbnail of this page in the Pages section of the Pages studio on the left-hand side. Click on it so that the full thumbnail is selected.

It should be fairly obvious which one it is because of where the text ends on the left-hand page. (When it isn't that obvious I will sometimes format my chapter header first to make it more obvious.)

You can also use the page numbers to find the correct spread. Because I haven't yet had you change the page numbering for this section of the document—something you will need to do—the page numbers you see in the main workspace should still match those in the Pages section, so that's another option as well.

So find the page spread you need to change, right-click on the thumbnail in the Pages section, and choose Apply Master from the dropdown menu.

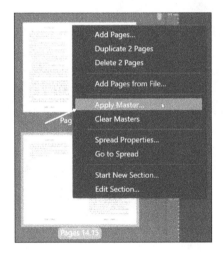

This will bring up the Apply Master dialogue box:

Click on the dropdown arrow next to the first master page name at the top of the dialogue box and choose the master page you want to apply. In this case Text and Chapter Start. Then click OK.

(This is why I like to order my master pages. Because once you have a decent number of them it makes it easier to find the one you want if they're in an intuitive order. For others, moving them to be alphabetical might work better. And some may just enjoy the chaos of leaving them as is.)

Here's that same two-page spread with the new master page applied. All I did was apply the master page, I didn't have to move the text down the page or anything like that. Applying the master page did that for me.

See how it added in our image and dropped the text down to where we want a chapter to start? Now all you need to do is apply the chapter heading style (Shift + 1) and the first paragraph style (Shift + 2) and this page is good to go.

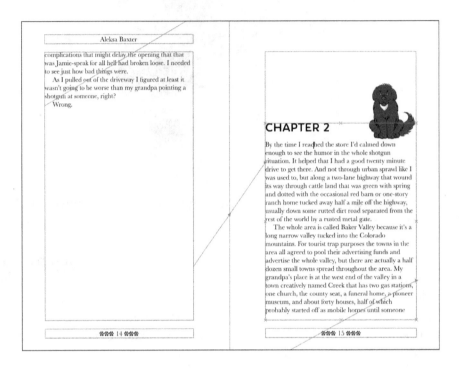

Although, that did create a widowed last line that continues onto the next page. So let's talk about strategies for manually fixing widows and orphans next.

MANUALLY FIX WIDOWS AND ORPHANS

If you chose not to have Affinity automatically fix your widows and orphans then you're going to need to fix them manually yourself. That's what I prefer to do because it gives me more control and lets my text be level at the bottom of each page.

The way I try to remove widows and orphans is by adjusting the tracking on that paragraph or surrounding paragraphs that will impact the one I'm trying to fix.

Tracking is located in the Positioning and Transform section of the Character studio. It is the second option on the left-hand side with an arrowed line under the letters VA.

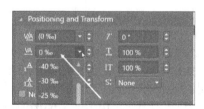

There is a dropdown there and what I generally do is try to tighten up a paragraph enough to bring the text in that paragraph up one line.

I try not to take this value past about -20% or so. I don't want the difference in the spacing to be noticeable to my readers. But if you're using justified text sometimes there can be big jumps because of a large word that was hanging up the paragraph so -25% can sometimes look better than -20%.

Let me show you an example. Here I have a two-page spread where there is the end of a paragraph stranded at the top of the page:

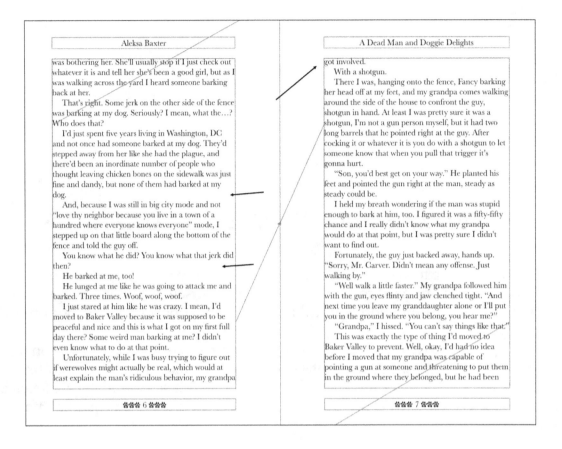

If I look back to the page before that line, I can see that I have two paragraphs on that prior page that end with short words.

One paragraph ends with just "dog." and one ends with just "then?" Both are good candidates for fixing this issue. (And honestly I might want to fix them just because ending a paragraph with a three-letter word is borderline bad formatting. Two-letter word, definitely bad. Three-letter, discretionary.)

What I do next is go to the paragraph that ends with that small word and try to adjust the tracking to see if it will pull that word up to the prior line.

In this case, changing the tracking to -5% for the paragraph that ended with "dog." was enough to bring that paragraph up one line. That eliminated my widow. But I decided to take it to -10% because it looks even better at -10%.

See?

Aleksa Baxter

was bothering her. She'll usually stop if I just check out whatever it is and tell her she's been a good girl, but as I was walking across the yard I heard someone barking back at her.

That's right. Some jerk on the other side of the fence was barking at my dog. Seriously? I mean, what the…? Who does that?

I'd just spent five years living in Washington, DC and not once had someone barked at my dog. They'd stepped away from her like she had the plague, and there'd been an inordinate number of people who thought leaving chicken bones on the sidewalk was just fine and dandy, but none of them had barked at my dog.

And, because I was still in big city mode and not "love thy neighbor because you live in a town of a hundred where everyone knows everyone" mode, I stepped up on that little board along the bottom of the fence and told the guy off.

You know what he did? You know what that jerk did then?

He barked at me, too!

He lunged at me like he was going to attack me and barked. Three times. Woof, woof, woof.

I just stared at him like he was crazy. I mean, I'd moved to Baker Valley because it was supposed to be peaceful and nice and this is what I got on my first full day there? Some weird man barking at me? I didn't even know what to do at that point.

Unfortunately, while I was busy trying to figure out if werewolves might actually be real, which would at least explain the man's ridiculous behavior, my grandpa got involved.

❦❦❦ 6 ❦❦❦

A Dead Man and Doggie Delights

With a shotgun.

There I was, hanging onto the fence, Fancy barking her head off at my feet, and my grandpa comes walking around the side of the house to confront the guy, shotgun in hand. At least I was pretty sure it was a shotgun, I'm not a gun person myself, but it had two long barrels that he pointed right at the guy. After cocking it or whatever it is you do with a shotgun to let someone know that when you pull that trigger it's gonna hurt.

"Son, you'd best get on your way." He planted his feet and pointed the gun right at the man, steady as steady could be.

I held my breath wondering if the man was stupid enough to bark at him, too. I figured it was a fifty-fifty chance and I really didn't know what my grandpa would do at that point, but I was pretty sure I didn't want to find out.

Fortunately, the guy just backed away, hands up. "Sorry, Mr. Carver. Didn't mean any offense. Just walking by."

"Well walk a little faster." My grandpa followed him with the gun, eyes flinty and jaw clenched tight. "And next time you leave my granddaughter alone or I'll put you in the ground where you belong, you hear me?"

"Grandpa," I hissed. "You can't say things like that."

This was exactly the type of thing I'd moved to Baker Valley to prevent. Well, okay, I'd had no idea before I moved that my grandpa was capable of pointing a gun at someone and threatening to put them in the ground where they belonged, but he had been slipping lately, and I'd been worried about him all

❦❦❦ 7 ❦❦❦

No more paragraph that ends with a short word and no more stranded final line of a paragraph.

Sometimes it isn't possible to fix it easily and then you just have to live with it. But often larger paragraphs or paragraphs with short words on the last line can be adjusted without the reader noticing the difference.

FIX JUSTIFIED PARAGRAPH ISSUES

If you chose to format your paragraphs as left justified you may run into a few other formatting issues you need to deal with. Basically, keep an eye out for paragraphs that stretched too much so that there's noticeable white space between words where there shouldn't be.

I can usually fix this by adjusting the tracking on that paragraph like I do for orphans and widows. Sometimes it's just a matter of pushing things together a little so that a big word moves up to the prior line.

Your other option that I mentioned briefly before is to apply hyphenation. Even if you don't want to use it for the whole book, you may want to apply it to a single paragraph, because if you have an especially long word that's causing the issue you may not be able to fix it with tracking.

Hyphenation is in the Paragraph studio. Just watch out if you do use hyphenation for a situation I believe is called pig bristles, where you have too much hyphenation in one paragraph. You can change the maximum consecutive hyphens setting to fix that.

CREATE MORE MASTER PAGES

For those of you getting ahead of me, you've probably realized we have an issue that we're going to run into soon. And that is what to do with a chapter that starts on the left-hand page like this one here:

We do not have a master page that will work in this situation. We have a Text and Chapter Start master page, but no master page for when the Chapter Start falls on the left-hand side.

You have a choice to make. Do you want your chapters to start wherever they fall, in which case this page will need a Chapter Start and Text master page? Or do you want all of your chapters to start on the right-hand page, in which case this page will need a No Text and Chapter Start master page?

In fiction, either one works. I've seen both in trade published books. In non-fiction and short story collections I have a strong preference for starting each chapter or story on the right-hand page.

In my novels I let my chapters start on whichever side of the page they happen to fall. With POD printing that can save you a few cents and usually my books are long enough I don't feel the need to stretch out their page count.

If you have an especially short title though, you may want to stretch it out a bit by starting all of your chapters on the right-hand side. Same is true of really short chapters. It starts to feel weird when all of the chapters are starting on the left-hand side of the page.

Either way, we don't have that master page so we need to go create a new one. Good news is, you can create new master pages at any point in time and it's not going to be a problem with your workflow. You won't have to go back and fix anything you've already done.

Let's create both, shall we?

NO TEXT AND CHAPTER START
MASTER PAGE

The No Text and Chapter Start master page is incredibly easy to create. It looks like this:

To create it, go to the Master Pages section of the Pages studio and copy the Text and Chapter Start master page. (Right-click, Duplicate, Rename).

Be sure to double-click on the renamed thumbnail before you start working.

Click on the Move Tool. Then click on every element (header, footer, text frame) on the left-hand page and delete it using the Delete key.

(You could also right-click and Cut each element or go to the Layers panel and right-click Cut or Delete or use the Delete key.)

Let's quickly apply that and our text styles to our Chapter 4 spread to see what it looks like:

Perfect. Because we removed the text box from the left-hand side of the spread, the text instead flowed straight to the right-hand page. And the left-hand page is entirely blank. That's exactly what we wanted for a right-hand chapter start.

CHAPTER START AND TEXT MASTER PAGE

Next, let's create the Chapter Start and Text master page.

Go back to the Master Pages section. We have to change a lot on this one, but the Text and Chapter Start master page is a good place to start. So Duplicate, Rename, double-click.

First step is to change the size of the text frames. Click on the left-hand text frame and in the Transform studio change the height to the height you've been using for your chapter starts, so in my case 4.75. Click and drag the text frame so that it's aligned with the bottom of the text area.

(The reason to change the text frame heights rather than click and drag them to the other page is because of the text flow issues that would create that I mentioned above. If you do click and drag, you will then need to remove the text flow and redo it so that the text still flows from the left-hand page to the right-hand page.)

Second step is to change the height of the text frame on the right-hand page. That's a simple click on the top line and drag upward to the top of the text area.

Next, click and drag the image from the right-hand page to the left-hand page. Be sure before you move the image that you checked its Y value in the Transform studio so that you can position the image at the same height on the left-hand page as it had on the right-hand page. So you want the Y value the same and you want to align the image along the right-hand edge of the text frame on the left-hand page.

After that, it's just fixing the header. We want to delete the Author Name header on the left-hand page and add a Title header on the right-hand page. There are a couple ways to do this.

Sometimes you can go to another master page, copy an element and paste it into your new master page and it will paste in at the exact same spot on the second master page. So in this case, I could go to the Text and Text master page, click on the Title header, Ctrl + C, come back to this master page, Ctrl + V. And if I'm lucky it will paste in at the exact location I need it.

I can then just delete the Author header element.

If that doesn't work but it did paste in, you can then click and drag it to align with the Author header and the main text frame on the right-hand page before you delete the Author header.

Your other option would be to copy your Author header, drag the copy into place, then delete the original Author header, and change out the field for Author to Title.

Leaving the Author header up allows you to easily align the headers. If you don't want to copy you can get the Y coordinate from the Transform studio first and then position your new header that way.

Whatever way you prefer.

When you're done and apply the master page and your text styles, this is what you should see, a chapter that starts on the left-hand page and then the rest of the chapter flowing from there:

CHAPTER 4

The day before the store opening dawned blue and beautiful, like most days in spring in the Colorado mountains. Fortunately for me, the last two weeks had passed without any exploding stoves or reports of my grandpa pointing a shotgun at someone new. I'd spent most of the time with Fancy, Jamie, and Katie Cross—who'd grown on me some, but not much—getting the store ready for our opening.

Luke had come through for us, just like Jamie said he would. He was still an over-the-top flirtatious sleazeball who was going to break my best friend's heart—again—but at least by the day before the opening we had a fully-functional store that didn't show a single sign of fire damage.

I had plans that day to go into the store and make sure everything was perfect for our launch, but not until after noon. Poor Fancy had put up with a lot of long hours sleeping in her nook at the store and I figured she'd earned a little hike in the woods before opening day.

Not that I really thought she minded all that time snoring away in the corner. She is a Newfie after all and

✳✳✳ 30 ✳✳✳

A Dead Man and Doggie Delights

Newfs aren't exactly the most energetic of breeds. But I knew she also liked to get out and smell new things and we really hadn't had a chance to do so since our arrival.

So after I fed her breakfast at five-thirty in the morning—an unfortunate side effect of living those first crucial months of her life in an apartment with a neighbor who had a loud alarm and liked to get up at that time every morning of every day—we headed up the mountain behind my grandpa's house.

Most of the mountainside was covered not only with big evergreens and tightly-clustered aspens, but with juniper bushes and long grass that you wouldn't want to try to walk through. Fortunately for us, there was a nice little trail I'd seen Mr. Jackson tending the day of our arrival that was just wide enough for me and Fancy to walk side-by-side. Mr. Jackson had done a good job of cutting back the branches, because not one slapped me in the face as we made our way towards the ridgeline about five hundred feet above my grandpa's house.

Fancy's a good girl so she didn't pull on her leash at all, just stopped to sniff and pee on things every few feet. She sometimes became a little too focused on one spot or another and I had to tell her to leave it and give a slight tug to move along, but usually I just let her do her thing. The walk was as much for her as it was for me, after all.

It was a gorgeous late spring morning. Birds were singing in the trees, bees were buzzing around on the early wildflowers scattered along the mountainside, and everything smelled fresh and clean and alive.

I was winded within five minutes because I wasn't used to hiking up mountainsides, and certainly not at

✳✳✳ 31 ✳✳✳

Now that you have everything you need, go through the whole document and apply your styles and master pages and any other adjustments.

FIX MISSING ITALICS OR BOLDED TEXT

Once you've gone through the whole document and applied your text styles, master pages, and fixed fiddly text issues, you will have a few more little things to fix.

If you applied a style like I did at the beginning using Ctrl + A and then Shift + 3, it is likely that you erased any italics or bolding that was applied to individual words within your paragraphs. I had you wait until now to fix those because if you needed to change the paragraph style on any of those paragraphs again (like for a first paragraph) you would've erased the formatting again and probably wouldn't have noticed a missed italics a second time.

A rare, but not impossible situation.

So now that you've made it through the whole document and your first paragraph styles are applied you can use Find to fix any missing italics or bold.

Go back to your source document and search for all entries with italics in them. (In Word, pull up the Find and Replace dialogue box and then type Ctrl + I in the Find What field to search for all italic entries.) You'll then have to manually go to your file in Affinity and search for those words to add the italics to each one using the Find and Replace studio. You can use Ctrl + I to apply italics to highlighted text.

As you do so, keep an eye out for if this shifts any paragraph. If so, I'd use Tracking to fix it.

If you have a lot of italics in your document or whole sentences or paragraphs, you may want to fix this earlier in your process because italics do take up a different amount of space than the plain text version. So maybe fix that first before you walk through the document. But keep in mind that if you have to apply a text style that you'll need to re-fix it. Another option might be to use a slightly different font size for the italics to make up for that difference.

(I just applied italics to a ten-line paragraph and it turned it into a nine-line paragraph. Tracking of 10% pushed it back to ten lines as did a font size of 13 pt instead of 12 pt.)

One more issue to note. Affinity has a flaw in its Find and Replace function. Find does not appear to work if there's an apostrophe in a word. So if you need to find the word "that's" in the phrase "That's what I was missing" to apply italics, you're going to need to search for "what I was missing" because searching for "that's" will return no result.

(This is one of those issues that could be fixed in a future update, so no harm in testing it each time they update to see if you still need a workaround.)

ASSIGN A PAGE ONE

We're almost done, but right now our first page of our main body of the novel is numbered 5.

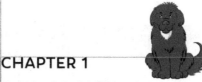

CHAPTER 1

I hadn't been in the Baker Valley a day before the trouble began.

Fancy—that's my three-year-old Newfoundland, full name Miss Fancypants—and I were sitting out back in the yard at my grandpa's reading a book and minding our own business, enjoying the mid-spring day.

Well, I was reading. Fancy was curled up nearby, her head on her paws, watching the world go by. Not that there was much of a world to see. My grandpa's place is on the edge of town and backs up to a mountainside covered in tall evergreens and aspen trees, so all she really had to see was five hundred feet of trees followed by an incredibly blue sky without a cloud in sight.

Man, I love Colorado.

Anyway. There we were, minding our own business, not bothering a soul, when Fancy jumped up and raced to the fence, barking like a mad woman. And it wasn't her "Hey, is that a dog, can we play?" bark either. It was her, "There's a jerk too close to my home" bark.

I reluctantly set my book aside—I'd just gotten to the good part, too—and dragged myself over to see what

🐾🐾 5 🐾🐾

We don't want that. We want it to be numbered 1. Changing this doesn't affect the flow of the text through the rest of the document which is why you didn't need to fix it before this. And leaving it as is meant that your on-screen page number would continue to match the page number shown in the Pages section of the Pages studio which made it easier to find your page spreads on the left-hand side when you needed to apply a new master page.

(I actually usually fix it earlier because it annoys me, but realized as I was writing this book that leaving it as is until the end was the better approach.)

Okay.

The reason Chapter 1 currently starts on page 5 is because right now we don't have separate sections in our document and that first chapter starts on the fifth page in the overall document. Affinity doesn't know any better so it's just numbering from the beginning.

To fix this, go to the Pages section of the Pages studio and click on the page that has Chapter 1 on it. You only want that page, not the page spread. So click on the page itself, not the name of the page spread.

You'll know you've done this correctly when just that one page is surrounded by a blue box.

Right-click and choose Start New Section. This will bring up the Section Manager dialogue box.

You can see on the left-hand side of the dialogue box that the document now has two sections and that Section 2 is selected and starts on page 5 of the overall document.

What we want to do here is to check the box for Restart Page Numbering At and then tell it to restart at 1. That's all we should have to do to fix this. Click Close.

And now the first page of the first chapter of the book should be numbered 1 even though it's the fifth page in the overall document.

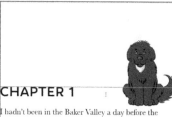

(If you ever need to do this for a book that has front matter that uses a different numbering style you may also need to change the numbering style to 1, 2, 3, 4 but we didn't need that here.)

TIDY UP

When you reach the end of the pages that Affinity added for you, you'll either have blank page spreads at the end because you changed the paragraph formatting after Affinity flowed your text for you and that new formatting didn't require as many pages.

Or you'll have a red circle or red arrow along the edge of the last text frame on your last page (and actually you'll see it throughout the whole document) because as you added chapter starts and chapter header formatting that pushed the text down enough to require more pages than Affinity added for you.

For me, I have extra pages.

It's easy enough to delete all of these. Just click on the bottom one, scroll up to the next to last one that's blank, hold down the Shift key and click on it, too. That should select all page spreads between the two.

Now right-click and choose Delete X Pages from the dropdown menu where X is the number of pages in the selected range.

Done. The page spreads are gone.

(The reason we left that last one there is because you still need an About the Author page.)

If you don't have enough pages, then you just need to tell Affinity to reflow your document again. So go to that right-hand edge of that last text frame on that last page, click on the red circle to turn it into a red arrow, hold down the Shift key and click on the red arrow. Affinity should flow the remaining text to new page spreads for you. Finish formatting those new pages and then it's time for back matter.

(Remember that Affinity will use the format of that last page spread when it reflows text, so you may want to change that last page spread to a Text and Text master page first if it wasn't already.)

ADD BACK MATTER

After the main body of your document, you're going to need to add back matter.

For all of my books I at least have an About the Author page in the back. For my YA fantasy series I also included a glossary of names and a glossary of terms. For books two and three in that series I include a synopsis of the prior books.

For non-fiction I often include an index.

So what you do next is really going to depend on what you want for your back matter. In this book I am just going to walk you through how to add a simple About the Author page. At this point you should know how to create new master pages for whatever you need.

Just remember that for sections after the main body text you continue the page numbering from the main body. So if the main text ends on page 199, your Index will be numbered 201.

You have three potential scenarios that can happen at this point.

First, the last chapter ends on the right-hand side of the spread, so you put your back matter text on the right-hand side of the next page. That requires a No Text and Section Start master page.

Second, the last chapter ends on the left-hand side of the spread and you put your back matter on the right-hand side of that same spread. This requires a Text and Section Start master page.

Third, the last chapter ends on the left-hand side of the spread, but you leave that right-hand page blank and start the back matter on the right-hand side of the next page. This requires a Text and No Text master page as well as a No Text and Section Start master page.

We're going to build master pages for the last scenario which also covers the first scenario.

TEXT AND NO TEXT
MASTER PAGE

To create a Text and No Text master page, go to the Master Pages section of the Pages studio and copy and rename the Text and Text master page. Be sure to double-click on your Text and No Text master page before making changes.

Select the Move Tool. Click on each element (header, footer, text frame) on the right-hand side of the spread and delete them.

If needed, click on the master page thumbnail and drag it down to the end of the master pages listing.

NO TEXT AND SECTION START MASTER PAGE

In the Master Pages section of the Pages studio, copy the No Text and Chapter Start master page, rename, double-click on the thumbnail to make sure you're editing the right one.

Click on the Move Tool. Delete the footer.

Click and drag the master page to the end of the master pages listing.

FINALIZE BACK MATTER

Once you have your back matter master pages created, assign them to the appropriate page spreads and add in any text you may need, such as the About the Author text. Apply your text styles to that text.

(I ended up tweaking the leading for the About the Author text because it went onto two lines and was too far apart for my liking. Because all of my chapter starts are one line I should be able to safely update the chapter header style to accommodate that, but I'd want to double-check the rest of the document after making that change to confirm.)

If you need more pages to add your back matter you can always right-click on the last page spread in the Pages section of the Pages studio and choose Add Pages.

Also, if Affinity is linking the about the author text frame to the main body text frames, which can sometimes happen but shouldn't, you can insert a break by clicking on the Artistic Text Tool, clicking into the text where you want the break, going to Text in the top menu, choosing Insert, Breaks, and then Frame Break or Page Break. Or you can unlink the frames by clicking on the blue arrow from the right-hand edge of the last frame in the main body of the document and clicking back into that same text frame. That should break the link.

Okay, so once you've done that, for the simple back matter we're doing here, you should have something similar to this.

A few more quick notes. Because the about the author section is going to be the same in each book we could have put that text into the master page spread instead.

If you do need to unlink the about the author text from the main body of the document, do it before you paste in the about the author text because otherwise it will be pulled back into the last frame of the main body of your document. (You'll see that little red circle or arrow indicating text that's hidden.)

And if you try to type * * * into Affinity it tries to turn that into a bulleted list. So if you're typing that within Affinity itself, leave out the spaces initially and then add them in after.

Okay. We're close. Just a few more steps to go.

PREFLIGHT

Your document at this point should be ready to export to PDF and review. But there's one more thing you can do and that's look at Preflight to check for any issues Affinity may have identified.

We put that studio on the top left at the end, so go click on it now.

The top entries relate to your master pages and are indicated with an M in the right-hand column. The entries below that are for your actual document.

For fiction most of what you'll see are spelling errors. I spellcheck outside of Affinity (and you should have certainly done so before this point because a change now could change your layout) so I generally ignore the spelling issues it flags. I'll glance at them, just in case, but especially in fiction I use a lot of words that spellcheck doesn't like (as you can see).

But you see that it did flag XXXX as a spelling error. That's my personal reminder that I need to update my copyright information with my actual values before this file is ready.

There are other helpful issues that Preflight flags such as images that are out of proportion, tables of contents that need updated, and overflowing text frames. So always be sure to scan the list. Anything flagged in red (like an overflowing text frame), as opposed to yellow like the items in the screenshot above, will prompt Affinity to ask you if you want to review Preflight before you export.

I'm not going to cover it here, but you can also customize what Preflight flags. I've customized the DPI it uses to alert for images, for example.

Anyway. It's always worth a glance although I mostly use it on the non-fiction side. I mention it because if Affinity ever suggests you look at it before export, you really should.

EXPORT A PDF

When you think the book is ready to go it's time to create the PDF file. To do this, go to File and then Export. This will bring up the Export Settings dialogue box. Click on PDF.

The single-most-important thing you need to do here is to change that dropdown for Area to All Pages instead of All Spreads.

(This is for people who are publishing via Amazon KDP or IngramSpark. I don't know if there are other printers out there where you don't need to do that, but for self-publishers it's absolutely crucial to make that change or you'll end up with a document that only prints half of your pages.)

And further to that point, when the PDF generates, make sure that the page count it shows is the same as the pages count in your Pages section of your Pages studio.

If you're doing a basic print book without a substantial number of images, you can use the Preset that's called PDF/X-1a:2003. That's the one IngramSpark says they like and it works just fine for Amazon as well. The Raster DPI should change to 300 when you do that.

For non-fiction I actually use a custom setting because I want to convert my images to grayscale before I submit to IngramSpark. Honestly, I have submitted files that had color images and they handled it just fine, but their recommendation is that you convert to grayscale first. For what we did here, I don't think it's something to worry about, but if you need that click on More down at the bottom to bring up a number of additional choices.

Once you've chosen your preset and changed the Area dropdown, click the box for Preview Export When Complete if it's not already checked. It should look like this now:

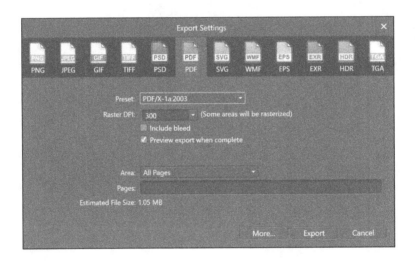

Click on Export.

Tell Affinity where to save the file and the name to use. Always verify the location you are saving your file.

(Do not assume that because the Affinity file you've been working on is saved to a specific folder that you will be exporting your finished file to that same location, because that's not how it works. Affinity exports to the last place you exported any Affinity file. I cannot count the number of times I've been caught out by that little fact.)

Click Save. Affinity will export the file and open it for you.

(I don't pay for a PDF program. My exported file opens in Adobe Acrobat Reader which I believe is free to use. When I was using Word and had images in my files I did run into an issue where the PDF export from Word wasn't high quality enough and I had to actually go to the paid Adobe site to convert my Word files to PDF to get the best quality for my images, but I haven't found that to be an issue working with Affinity Publisher.)

First things first, check the page count. It should match the page count in the Pages section of the Pages studio. If it doesn't, you probably need to re-export.

Next, scroll through the document page by page and make sure everything looks okay.

Are the headers and footers aligned? Do they include the full text they should? Are your paragraphs uniformly formatted? Did you catch all of the chapter starts and format them correctly and assign the proper master page?

If there are images in the file, do they look okay? (If at any point you move a linked image or rename it Affinity will show a blurred space where that image should be instead of the image itself.)

It's easier to check for extra pages or chapters or sections that start on the wrong side in Affinity itself using the Pages section of the Pages studio because of how it's laid out, but you can look for that here, too.

Make sure that any default fields, like Author Name, have been completed with the actual author name. And ISBN has been added in place of XXXX, etc. If you're changing out the image, make sure you did so and that it worked for all of the master pages that use that image. Make sure the Author and Title at the top of each page are the correct ones.

Check for italics and bolding in your main body text that might have been lost when you applied your paragraph styles.

Basically, does it look "right"?

If you do have to make any changes, then you'll need to export a new copy and review everything again.

REUSE AN OLD BOOK

As I mentioned before, when it comes time to publish a new book in a series I tend to just take my last book in that series, save a copy of the file under the new title, delete out the old content, and use that file to create the next book in the series.

If you're going to do that, it is very important that you really delete out the old text. To do so, go to the main body of your document and use Ctrl + A to select all of the text in the main body of the document and then delete it.

If you have even one linked text frame left, just deleting pages that have text showing in them DOES NOT get rid of the text itself. You have to select and delete the text before you delete the pages displaying that text.

After I delete the text I usually then delete all of the pages back to that initial set-up of seven pages we had when we flowed our text. So I leave the title page, also by, copyright and chapter start, and my first text and text spread. I then change all of my front matter for the new book and drop in the main body text of that new book and have Affinity flow it to new pages for me and then format.

I find that this is the easiest way to have all of the master pages and text styles I need. (You can copy in text styles and master pages from other Affinity files, but this was the easiest option I found. I also did try the Affinity template option at one point. It didn't work for me. I find this approach to be far easier.)

CONCLUSION

Alright. That's it. That's the basics of how to use Affinity Publisher to format a fiction title. Non-fiction, as I've alluded to a few times, can be much more complex. Especially if you try to add an index; I've found that part to be especially buggy and it's crashed my program more than once.

But for a basic fiction title, once you get those master pages set up the first time, it's incredibly easy to use. I expect that you'll want to tweak things a bit and that's fine. You should have the basic skills you need now to do that. See the Appendix for the quick and dirty rundown of the skills we covered here if you do need a refresher on anything. (I'm always forgetting exactly how to flow text.)

Also, if you don't feel like building your own master pages or things went horribly wrong as you followed this book, I do have some templates available on my Payhip store for purchase. They're basically a blank version of the file we just created with the text styles set up to be easily swapped out for a new font.

And if it turns out you learn better via video or want to see what we covered here in video, I have also done a video version of this book that can be found at ml-humphrey.teachable.com. You can use discount code HALFOFF to get fifty percent off.

As always with everything that is writing-related but not writing itself, remember that the bells and whistles are nice, but creating more books is the most important way to achieve success in this business. So don't let formatting your books distract you from creating more books. (Like I do far too often.)

Having said that, learning a skill like this can have tremendous benefits. It didn't work for all of my books, but being able to put together large print editions of my titles at no additional cost other than my time was a decision that has paid off nicely for me. Compare that to the time it takes to write a whole novel and sometimes the time spent better leveraging what you already have can be worth it.

Anyway.

If you have any questions, feel free to reach out at mlhumphreywriter@gmail.com. Good luck with it!

* * *

And if you're interested in learning more advanced print formatting techniques like how to insert tables of contents or indexes or how to merge multiple titles together, then check out *Affinity Publisher for Non-Fiction* which is available as a book or a video course.

APPENDIX A: QUICK TAKES

AUTHOR NAME

FIELD EDIT

Fields studio. Click on field next to Author. Type author name. Enter.

INSERT

Artistic Text Tool. Click on location in document where field should be inserted. Go to Fields studio. Double-click on Author.

BOOK TITLE

FIELD EDIT

Fields studio. Click on field next to Title. Type book title. Enter.

INSERT

Artistic Text Tool. Click on location in document where field should be inserted. Go to Fields studio. Double-click on Title.

IMAGE

INSERT

Place Image Tool. Select image to insert. Open. Image may automatically insert. If not, click and drag in workspace until desired size.

INSERT IN PICTURE FRAME

Click on picture frame layer. Place Image Tool. Select image to insert. Open. Image will insert in frame.

MOVE

Move Tool. Click on image layer or directly on image if not in a picture frame. Click on image, hold left-click and drag to desired location. Use snapping to align along edges or center.

REPLACE

Document top menu option. Resource Manager. Select image. Replace. Select new image. Open. Close resource manager.

RESIZE

Move Tool. Click on image layer or directly on image if not in a picture frame. Option A: Transform studio. Lock Aspect Ratio. Change height or width value. Option B: Click on blue circle in corner and drag at an angle to resize proportionately. Or click on blue circle along any edge to change height or width only. This will skew most images.

UNPIN

Layers studio. Click on image layer. Open Pinning studio. Click on Unpin.

MASTER PAGE

ADD NEW

Pages studio. Master Pages section. Right-click on existing master page. Option A: Choose Insert Master. Click OK to create a new master page that has the basic properties of the existing master page. Option B: Choose Duplicate to create an exact duplicate of the existing master page.

MOVE

Pages studio. Master Pages section. Click on master page and drag. Blue line along edge will show where master page will move to. Release left-click when where wanted.

RENAME

Pages studio. Master pages section. Click on master page thumbnail. Click on name of master page. Type in new name. Enter.

NEW DOCUMENT PRESET

RENAME

Right-click on thumbnail for preset. Rename Preset. Type new name. OK.

PAGE NUMBER

INSERT

Artistic Text Tool. Click where you want page number placed. Text top menu choice. Insert. Fields. Page Number.

RESTART AT 1

Pages studio. Pages section. Click on page where you want to restart at 1. Right-click. Start New Section. (Or Edit Section if one has already been started.) Click button for Restart Page Numbering At. Enter 1. Confirm numbering style is correct. If not, choose the correct one from the dropdown menu.

CHANGE NUMBER STYLE

Pages studio. Pages section. Right-click on a page and choose Edit Section. Click on section name that contains the pages where you want to change the numbering style. Choose the new style from the Number Style dropdown menu. Close.

PAGES

ADD PAGES

Pages studio. Pages section. Right-click on an existing page or page spread. Add Pages. Choose the number of pages, whether to insert before or after, the page number (based on left-hand panel numbering where the pages should be inserted), and select the master page to use for the inserted pages. OK.

APPLY MASTER PAGE

Pages studio. Pages section. Right-click on the pages where you want to apply the master page. (Be sure that both pages are selected in a two-page spread. Apply Master. Choose desired master page from dropdown menu. OK.

DELETE PAGES

Pages studio. Pages section. Click on page spread that you want to delete. Right-click. Delete X Pages. If there is more than one page spread that you want to delete, click on page spread at one end of the page range, hold down the shift key and click on the page spread at the top of the page range. Right-click. Delete X Pages.

SECTION NAME

ASSIGN

Pages studio. Pages section. Right-click and Edit Section. In Section Manager, click on the section that you want to rename. Type name into Section Name field. Close.

INSERT

Click on location in header where field should be inserted. Go to Text top menu option. Insert. Fields. Section Name.

SNAPPING

ENABLE

Go to the horseshoe shaped magnet image in the top center. Click on the dropdown arrow. Check the box next to Enable Snapping.

STUDIO

MOVE OR ANCHOR

Left-click on studio tab and drag to desired location. To anchor, either drag until you see a blue box appear and then release or drag to where other studios are already anchored and add to those tabs.

STUDIO PRESET

ADD NEW

Arrange studios as desired. View top menu option. Studio Presets. Add Preset. Type name. OK.

APPLY

View top menu option. Studio Presets. Select desired preset. Or Ctrl + Shift + [Number].

DELETE

View top menu option. Studio Presets. Manage Studio Presets. Select preset name. Delete. Close.

RENAME

View top menu option. Studio Presets. Manage Studio Presets. Select preset name. Rename. Type in new name. OK. Close.

SAVE CHANGES

Make desired changes to studio preset arrangement. View top menu option. Studio Presets. Add Preset. Type in exact same name as before. OK. Agree to overwrite old preset.

TEXT

ADD SPECIAL SYMBOLS OR CHARACTERS

Artistic Text Tool. Click into workspace where desired. Go to View top menu. Studio. Glyph Browser. Or if docked, open glyph browser. Find desired symbol or character. Double-click on symbol or character to insert.

ADD SPACE BETWEEN LINES

Artistic Text Tool. Select paragraph of text. Paragraph studio. Spacing section. Leading dropdown. Choose desired option. Or for multiple lines of the same style, click on Space Between Same Styles and set a value.

ALIGNMENT

Artistic Text Tool. Click on the paragraph or paragraphs. Menu choices above workspace. Four images with lines. Align Left, Align Center, Align Right, or dropdown menu for Justify Left, Justify Center, Justify Right, Justify All, Align Towards Spine, Align Away From Spine. Or, to the right of that, dropdownmenu for Top Align, Center Vertically, Bottom Align, Justify Vertically. The horizontal alignment options are also available at the top of the Paragraph studio.

ALL CAPS OR SMALL CAPS

Artistic Text Tool. Select the text to be formatted. Go to Character studio. Typography section. Click on the two capital Ts (TT) to apply all caps. Click on the capital T with a smaller capital T (TT) to apply small caps.

APPLY HYPHENATION

Artistic Text Tool. Select text. Paragraph studio. Hyphenation section. Click on box next to Use Auto-Hyphenation. Change values as needed.

APPLY TRACKING

Artistic Text Tool. Select text. Character studio. Positioning and Transform section. Second option in the left-hand column, Tracking. Click arrow for dropdown menu. Choose desired change.

BOLD

Artistic Text Tool. Select text. Ctrl + B. Or click on B in top menu. Or go to Character studio and choose the Strong option from the Style dropdown menu at the top. Only works if there is a bold version of the font available.

FONT

Artistic Text Tool. Select text. Top menu, left-hand side. Font dropdown. Choose font. Or select text and go to Character studio font dropdown at top.

INDENT PARAGRAPH

Artistic Text Tool. Select paragraph. Paragraph studio. Spacing section. Second option on left-hand side. (First Line Indent). Add value.

KEEP TOGETHER

Artistic Text Tool. Select second paragraph or line that you want to keep together. Go to the Paragraph studio. Flow Options section. Check box for Keep With Previous Paragraph.

LINE SPACING (LEADING)

Artistic Text Tool. Select paragraph. Paragraph studio. Spacing section. Change value in Leading dropdown. Default is usually a good place to start.

ORPHANS REMOVE AUTOMATICALLY

Artistic Text Tool. Select text. Paragraph studio. Flow Options. Check box for Prevent Orphaned First Lines.

ITALICS

Artistic Text Tool. Select text. Ctrl + I. Or click on I in top menu. Or go to Character studio and choose the Emphasis option from the Style dropdown menu at the top. Only works if there is an italic version of the font available.

JUMP IMAGE

Move Tool. Select image. Click on Show Text Wrap Settings option in top menu. In Text Wrap dialogue box choose Jump as desired Wrap Style.

SIZE

Artistic Text Tool. Select text. Top menu, left-hand side. Font size dropdown. Choose size or type in size. Or select text and go to Character studio font size dropdown at top.

UNDERLINE

Artistic Text Tool. Select text. Ctrl + U. Or click on the underlined U in top menu. Or go to Character studio and choose one of the underlined U options from the Decorations section.

WEIGHT

Artistic Text Tool. Select text. Top menu, left-hand side. Font weight dropdown. Choose from available weights for that font. Or select text and go to Character studio font weight dropdown at top.

WIDOWS REMOVE AUTOMATICALLY

Artistic Text Tool. Select text. Paragraph studio. Flow Options. Check box for Prevent Widowed Last Lines.

WRAP AROUND IMAGE

Move Tool. Select image. Click on Show Text Wrap Settings option in top menu. In Text Wrap dialogue box choose Wrap Style.

TEXT FLOW

AUTO FLOW

Pages studio. Pages section. Double-click on last page spread in section. Go to right-hand edge of last text frame in workspace. Click on red circle to see red arrow. Hold down shift key and click on red arrow. Affinity will flow the text to as many page spreads as needed using the same master page spread format.

FROM ONE TEXT FRAME TO ANOTHER ADD

Click on blue arrow along the edge of the first text frame. Click on second text frame.

FROM ONE TEXT FRAME TO ANOTHER REMOVE

Click on the blue arrow along the edge of the first text frame. Click back onto the first text frame.

TEXT FRAME

ALIGN OR POSITION

Frame Text Tool or Move Tool. Left-click on text frame and hold as you drag. Look for red and green alignment lines to center or align to other elements in workspace. (Turn on Snapping if there are no red or green lines.)

INSERT

Frame Text Tool on left-hand side. Click and drag in workspace.

TEXT STYLE

APPLY

Artistic Text Tool. Select text. Use dropdown menu at top to apply style. Or go to Text Styles studio and click on desired style. Or use shortcut if one is associated with the style.

BASED ON OTHER STYLE

To base a text style off of another style, first apply the existing text style. Next, make any edits to create the new style. And then save as new style.

KEYBOARD SHORTCUT

For a new style, add keyboard shortcut in the Style section of the Create Paragraph Style dialogue box where it says Keyboard Shortcut. (Don't type the description, just use the shortcut when you're clicked into the box.) For an existing style, go to the Text Styles studio, right-click on the style name, Edit [Style Name], and then in the Style section of the Edit Text Style dialogue box, add the keyboard shortcut.

NEW

Artistic Text Tool. Select text. Format text. Text style dropdown in top menu. New Style. Give style a name and keyboard shortcut if desired. OK.

UPDATE OR CHANGE

Artistic Text Tool. Select text with style to be updated. Make edits. Click on paragraph symbol with a swish that's to the right of the text style dropdown menu in the top menu area. Or, go to Text Styles studio, right-click on text style name, Edit [Style Name], make edits in Edit Text Style dialogue box, OK.

APPENDIX B: CREATE A BOOK FROM AN EXISTING FILE

1. Delete out any old text from the main body of the existing file and delete all pages except the front matter, first chapter start page, and the first Text and Text page.

2. If you want to use different fonts in your document than are used in the existing file, change the fonts for the relevant text styles. If your document is set up with primary and secondary text styles then you only need to change the primary text style for each font.

3. Replace the image(s) in the document or delete the images from the master pages, if needed.

4. After you've replaced any image, make sure it is still positioned properly on each master page.

5. Edit the text on the Title page to reflect the correct book title.

6. Edit the text on the Also By page to reflect the correct author name, series name, and title name.

7. Edit the text on the Copyright page to show the copyright year, copyright name, and ISBN for the title.

8. Go to the Fields studio and edit the Author and Title fields to show the correct author name and book title.

9. Paste in the main body text of your document.

10. If your text imported with an assigned style or styles, you can use find and replace to change the assigned styles to the ones you need. Otherwise, apply the main body text style for now.

11. Flow your text by Shift + clicking on the red arrow on the right-hand edge of the right-hand text box of the last page which should be a Text and Text page.

12. Assign chapter header and paragraph text styles to the first page of the main body of the book. Double-check that the document looks good. That all images are placed properly, chapter starts are where you want them, paragraphs are formatted as desired, etc. If not, fix those issues in your master pages or text styles before proceeding.

13. Walk through your main body text and assign chapter header, first paragraph, and section break formatting to the text as needed. Also change the master page assigned for each spread when needed. And fix any widows, orphans, one-line chapter ends, etc.

14. At the end of the document you may need to either reflow the text again to cover all of your text and/or there may be extra pages that weren't used that need to be deleted.

15. Add your back matter. At a minimum this should include an About the Author page.

16. Export to PDF (PDF X-1a:2003 should work for most purposes) being sure to change the Area selection to All Pages from All Spreads.

17. Review the PDF file and verify that all pages exported and look as expected. Specifically check headers, footers, paragraph formatting, master page assignment, chapter header and section break formatting, front matter, and back matter. Also check for single-line chapter endings, widows, orphans, short words at the end of paragraphs, and too much white space in justified paragraphs.

18. For any issues, fix them in the Affinity file and then re-export and re-review. When final, the PDF should be ready to upload for printing.

INDEX

ABOUT THE AUTHOR

M.L. Humphrey is a self-published author with both fiction and non-fiction titles published under a variety of pen names. When she gets stuck on her next fiction project she foolishly decides to write books that only ten people are going to buy, although she does usually learn something interesting in the process so it's worth it in the end.

You can reach her at:

mlhumphreywriter@gmail.com

or at

www.mlhumphrey.com

www.ingramcontent.com/pod-product-compliance
Lightning Source LLC
Chambersburg PA
CBHW060136060326
40690CB00018B/3901